BABA

GOD IS LOVE
LIVE IN LOVE

COMPILED

BY

GRACE J. MC MARTIN

First Edition

Published by:
Sathya Sai Book Center of America
305 West First Street
Tustin, CA 92780-3108
USA

ISBN 1-57836-098-6

The Young Avatar

PREFACE

This is another book that has been put together from Baba's Discourses. Baba gave me His Permission, His Help and His Love. Without these it would not have been possible to do this work.

In this book are a few pieces taken from "A Recapitulation of Sathya Sai Baba's Divine Teachings." As in that book, this book contains most of Baba's discourses about Children, Mothers and Teachers. This book has been put together because of the increasing way that children have been mistreated today due to the lack of love for these lovely and pure-hearted children and also due to an absence of protection.

Twenty years ago the neglect of children and child abuse were largely hidden or unacknowledged problems. That is not true today! There is an increasing awareness of the creeping tide of this problem. You may ask where do we begin? AT HOME!

The first step for help and protection of the children has to start in the HOME. The mother is the best protector of all. How sad it is for a child when it comes home from school and finds an empty house! The mother is working or socializing and the father is very busy trying to make money to give his family more outward comfort but not the inward comfort of LOVE and CARE.

How is it possible for a child to grow well, straight and strong without paternal guidance? The growing problem of the children is so large now because people don't seek the root of the problem. The reason for the problem is quite clear. It is the absence of the MOTHER in the HOME. What use is there in having children if you are not going to bring them up? You will put your children in the hands of someone else to raise them.

This person will do the job for a living but most often without love. So the children lack, at that early age, the most essential health-giving Vitamin, the LOVE of the MOTHER.

At first this book was going to be about children but, because of the children's problems the parents and the teachers are involved. So if parents and teachers know their position relative to the children, the problem can be lessened.

In this book are Baba's discourses. His descriptions are not often known. Some are unaware of the real Beauty of Children, the Loveliness of Motherhood and the wonderful qualities that God has given to Women. As Baba says these things are not perceived by most of us.

So this book is about Children, Mothers and Teachers. But it is also about God and Love, as God and Love are the paramount components for helping with the children's problems and the world's problems.

According to Sai Baba the woman's position is not only in her home but in the whole world. Women have a special place in the world. The women determine whether a country will prosper or decline. Their acts and conduct are the crucial factor.

Let us pray that this problem will be solved with Baba's help and love. We believe that all children are everybody's responsibility. So all of us can help. As Baba says each one of us is like a tiny screw or bolt in the large wheel of the world.

Humble prostrations at Your Divine Lotus Feet in
gratitude for Your Help and Love.

Grace J. McMartin

DEAR READER

Since ancient times The Vedas have been proclaiming the profound Truth that all is One. The Truth is One. It has been hammering all is One to man since the beginning of time to awaken man to the discovery and realization of his real nature, the Self. He emerges from the Formless into form, merging from the form into the Formless. That is to say he realizes himself, that he is God.

Sometime in this book you will find repetition. But it is not merely a repetition, it is just simply a continuation of Baba's Teaching. It is necessary to repeat so that it will be absorbed by the resisting mind. Every time you read again it goes deeper and deeper by taking delight in the Word of God. By this means will arise love for God and non-attachment to the world. The sacred teaching of the Sages are ever new and ever inspiring. The truth is One, continuous, changeless and eternal.

So an amount of repetition perhaps will be necessary for the devotee to inquire and put in practice what he has read.

Baba

"I have been giving discourses for the past sixty years but you are not making any effort to put into practice at least a few of the teachings. It is rather surprising even to Me, that for the past few days I did not feel like speaking at all, as there was no marked change in you. I thought there was no point in continuing to speak to you. Hence I have decided to confine Myself to a few words, What do you except Me to speak? I have already taught all that ought to be taught. There is nothing more to convey. I am pained to see that my teachings have gone in vain and all My sweet words have become tasteless to you.

Devotees are not grateful for the Love and Grace showered on them by Swami.

October 14th, 1999 Discourses

Practice Bhagavan's Teachings

CONTENTS

ILLUSTRATIONS

MESSAGE

When a child is born, worry too is born with it—worry that it should grow up healthy and pure, learned and good, famous but humble, bringing a fair name to the parents and elders. I would advise you to postpone the celebration of the birth of a child, until the day it brings Sathkirthi (good fame) to the lineage and the country. Also, celebrate the accumulation of wealth when it is spent justly and with love, on beneficial and deserving purposes. A tree is justified by fragrant flowers bringing forth sweet fruits.

—BABA

An Avatar

Is

God Himself

Descending

In the Human Form

The

Blooming of

God

in Human Form

The Sweetness of God

At this age he threw off his books and declared I have My work waiting for Me

The Young Sathya Sai Baba

The old cobbler saw him seated in the hall and Baba asked what he wanted of Him. The cobbler said, "Please come to my house and accept something." Baba said, "All right, I shall come," and lovingly patted the cobbler's back. And He did come. Baba had made by His visit a place of pilgrimage for the entire neighborhood.

During this period He drew people to Him by means of mahimas (miracles) for as He has so often said, without these 'visiting cards' no one can gauge even a fraction of His glory.

He has emerged as the
Great Teacher of the people

On His visit to Rishikesh, Kashmir, Mathura, Baba announced His advent

Baba riding Raja in the Kashmir Valley

Baba Himself is the great musician

"The Same Sai Baba"
As a young boy Baba declared His identity

It was the day of Dasara in 1961 when Baba said that He had started the work for which He had come.

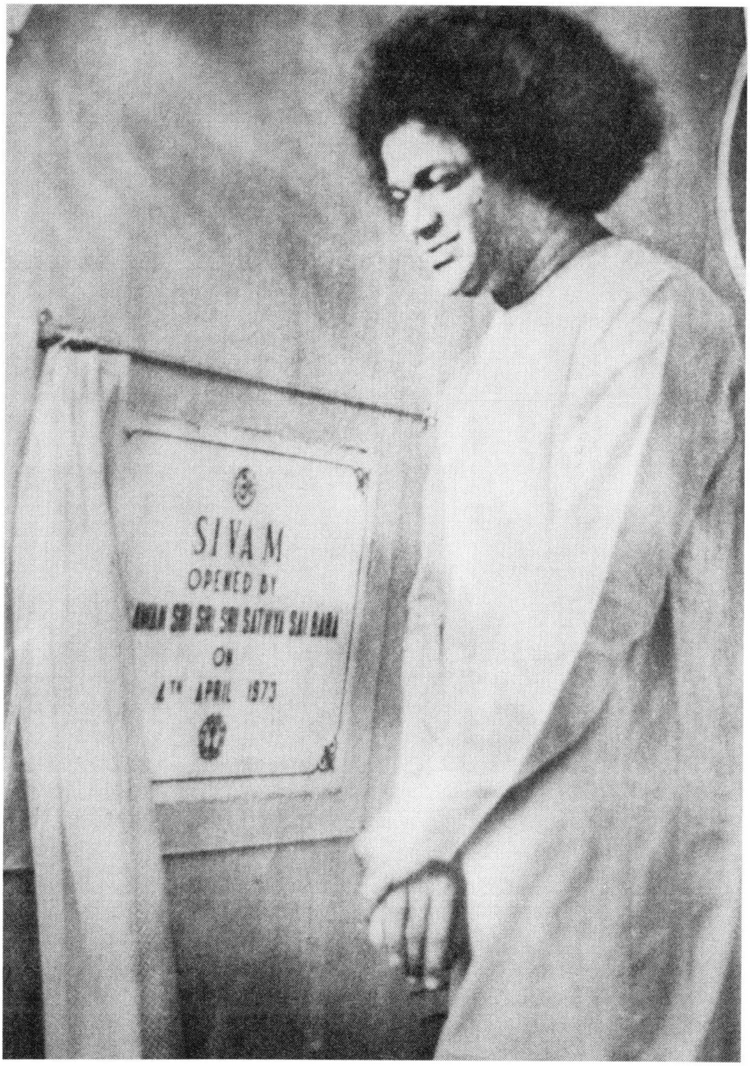

The opening of the Mandir
In Hyderabad in 1973

BABA SAYS

GOD is love,
So you must become Love in
order to merge with
Him.

GOD IS PRESENT

God is present, Now and at every Now
Though no eye has seen, He is everywhere.
To save the worlds from blinding night
He waves two lamps in space—the sun and moon.
He stays the million twinkling hordes of stars
Firm on firmament, lest they clash and crash.
He holds aloft the big blue dome so far above
With neither prop nor pillar from below.
He rotates our globe, so fast, in silent smooth
With never a jolt or jar, with even pace
He lovingly fans soft soothing breeze
With never a demand for wages and perks.
He has chained the feet of reckless raging seas
Lest they rush on land in ruinous haste.

God is present, now and at every Now
Though no eye has seen Him, what does He do?
From behind the curtain, He directs the Dance
That happens on stage, to the tune He wills.

—BABA

(Translation of a poem He sang during a recent discourse.)

BABA SAYS

God is Present in the

Core of your Heart

and everywhere.

WE CANNOT DESCRIBE GOD

God is the Inner Reality, ever present in All beings.

God is none other than the SELF.

To define God is to deny God. If we define God we are limiting the Limitless One. We are confining Him with the concepts of mind. God is beyond the reach of the gross mind, but He can be reached through Love with a pure subtle and one-pointed mind. Take refuge in God and constantly recite His Name.

God is to be recognized in all that exists.

The word God is the indication that there is God. If there was no God the word God would not have originated and gained currency. You may see God or you may not, but the word is proof that God is there.

We cannot describe God in the vocabulary learnt upon the earth. It is not possible for anyone to describe or understand the fullness and the total aspect of the Lord. We have to experience the Bliss of realizing Him as the core of our being.

He is in the very heart of every being.

God is in us, around us and beyond us; as the air is imperceptible in the absence of the breezes or of things that it moves; so God too can be known only by His manifestation in man and beast, plant and bird, in things and beings all around us. No one yet knows the mystery of the electric current, why it behaves so, what is the exact nature of the origin and flow; but, yet it is manipulated into a thousand uses and it is manifesting as a thousand appliances and instrument.

So too, God is present everywhere. But we can understand only that part of Him that manifest before our cognition. Ordinary people will swear that the Earth does not move at all; it is held forth in poetry as a symbol of stability. But it has two motions, both unbelievably fast! It rotates on its axis at a speed which exceeds a thousand miles per hour; even while rotating so the Earth moves round the Sun at an astonishing rate of speed! But do we notice it while it happens?

God too is a reality ever present in us and in every being; but we miss Him as we miss the movement of the earth.

We have to infer God through proofs and evidences of His Providence, His Grace, His majesty, His Glory.

Just as we infer the movements of the earth, the moon and the stars, by watching the sky, the seasons and the precise procession of day and night.

God is everywhere and in everyone. The whole Universe is inhabited by Him. One should find God in every object. These are the ideals we find in our scriptures. There are bulbs of different colors and their voltage also differs. But whatever the color and whatever the voltage, the current that flows is the same.

God is very much in the world, in and through everything in it, with no exception. In the Gita the Lord announces, I am man among living beings, the cow among animals, the lion among beast, the cobra among snakes, the eagle among birds. Prahlada among Rakshasas (evil spirit), etc. No item is discarded as not worthy of God. There is no body that He does nor activate; no Form that He does not reside in.

He is fragrance, brilliance, sweetness and taste, intelligence, valor, austerity, fame, contentment—all desirable things and qualities.

One can acquire unalloyed Bliss only by knowing the Universal All-inclusive Glory of the Lord.

God without Name and Form is the Essence of Reality.

God is the Eternal Witness

God is the Witness, the guide and guardian.

God alone is Eternal.

Man is a momentary flash, a tiny wavelet, that rises and falls.

Man is on a long pilgrimage towards God.

He moves from one life to another to the goal of Splendor.

God is the Embodiment of Eternal, Ever-full and Joy.

God is Eternal and Changeless.

You are the Full

You are God

The Cosmos was created by God out of Himself, so that He is the Originator as well as the material of the World.

As a result

He is Full. The Creation is also Full and the Individual Self is also Full.

So too

The Cosmos and All Creation are but the billion bodies of God.

He is All this and in All this, but, He is Changeless and Eternal.

God has to be experienced in His Fullness, and the Bliss of that experience made one's permanent possession.

God is Bliss and when God is the undying spring in you. You, will have Bliss

FOREVER

FULLNESS

Fullness means wholeness. Wholeness implies One and not two or three. There cannot then be any place for the individual. When the individual Self; the particularized differentiated Self, has become full and whole, there is no possibility of his return to the consciousness of the objective world.

When the individualized Self become fixed in the totality or the Whole he loses all ideas of distinction and is ever in the Consciousness of the totality. The One that subsumes the many. He will then be aware that the Reality of each is the reality of all and that Reality is the One Indivisible Self. He will not exhibit any consciousness of distinction between the individuals.

The Divine that he knows, as the core of each thing and being is now recognized by him as the Divine that he himself is; and he will be deeper than ever in the Fullness of Bliss. The rays of that Bliss illumine all regions.

BABA SAYS

Of all Virtues Love is the foremost It may be said that Love is a Universal Virtue and it is being manifest in human relations, more or less by all. If love is fostered, all other qualities flow from it. In every form of Spiritual discipline, Love has the first place. Love helps you to see God in everyone and everyone as Divine. Love of the Divine is the first requirement in the march toward the realization of one's humanness. Love is the supreme mark of humanness. There is nothing more precious than Love within human grasp. Intensify the Love that is within you as a sacred Gift. Expand it so that all beings can share in it. It is essential to cultivate the sense of Oneness. Love alone signifies that Oneness. For this Love there is no Path, no Reward, no Discipline, other than Love "Itself." The more you develop the Love the more you experience Bliss. So fill your entire life with Love. A life without Love is utterly barren.

BABA SAYS

MY LOVE IS MY GREATEST MIRACLE

All should share in this Love. Then it becomes one.

SWAMI'S LOVE

Will be with you always, in you, beside you and around you.

The Sages called it Self.

This Divine Flame of Love shines in every heart. Self and Heart are synonymous with Divinity. For this Love there in no distinction of "mine" and "thine." It is totally free from self-interest.

Love is like a mariner's compass, which always points to the north.

At any time, any place in any circumstance Love points only towards GOD.

Hence, everyone should try to understand how the Principle of Love works.

Love can be compared only with Love.

The Principle of Love in the greatest unifying force which unites all spiritual practices, all creeds, all goals of life and all scriptures.

LOVE BE YOUR VERY BREATH

Man's nature is Love. He cannot survive a moment, when deprived of Love. It is the very breath of his life. When the six vices, to which he was attached so long, disappear, Love is the only occupant of the Heart; but Love has to find an object, a

Loved one.

It cannot be alone.

So, it is directed to the dark-blue Divine Child, the charming cowherd Boy, who is Purity Personified, who is the Embodiment of service, sacrifice and self-less-ness, who has taken residence in the

Cleansed Altar.

There is no scope now for any other attachment to grow. So, step by step, this Love for God becomes deeper, purer, more self-denying, until at last, there is no other need for thought and the individual is merged in the

UNIVERSAL!

LOVE IS SWEETER THAN NECTAR

Love is the form of the Supreme (the Absolute). Love permeates the Absolute.

Only when Love is merged with love can God be attained. There is nothing greater than Love in the Cosmos.

Love is sweeter than Nectar.

It is because men have forgotten this Love that they have become a prey to all kinds of ills and lost peace of mind. Because men have lost the Love of God and fear of sin they have become veritable demons.

Man lost Divine love because of complete involvement in worldly things and ephemeral desires.

Nectar is described by the Scriptures as extremely sweet. But Nectar nowhere approaches the sweetness of Love. As against Love, Nectar appears insipid. The uniqueness of such Love is beyond the comprehension of ordinary people. Such Love arises only when you churn the Ocean of Bliss.

Hence, all our actions should be based on Love. But in this mundane world, Love assumes external forms. When pure gold is given to the goldsmith for making a jewel, he mixes copper and other metals with it and thereby its value is reduced.

Likewise, because pure Love is mixed with worldly attachments, it gets tainted. But when such tainted Love is directed towards service it gets purified.

However, when Love is directed towards God, it becomes pure, selfless, enduring and Divine.

WOMEN

IN WOMEN, DIVINITY EXISTS TO

A GREAT EXTENT

THE REPUTATION OF THE ENTIRE HOME

AND EVEN A WHOLE NATION DEPENDS ON

THE WOMAN

Women must be given education in a well-planned manner. Their mission is to lay down and canons of rightness and morality.

BABA SAYS

If the women of a country are happy, healthy and holy, the men of that country will be hardy, honest and happy, so woman has a very crucial role in individual and social uplift

WOMEN ARE ENTITLED TO UNIVERSAL RESPECT

Woman is considered as the Embodiment of the Goddess of energy. Women who are the repositories of the Embodiment of the Divine energy are in no way inferior: how full of fortitude, patience and love is their nature! Their self-control is seldom equaled by men. They are the exemplars and leaders, for men to tread the spiritual path. Pure selfless love is inborn in women.

The woman is the prop of the home and of religion. She plants and fosters religious faith or it dries up. Women have a natural aptitude for faith and spiritual endeavor. Women with devotion, faith, and meekness can lead men on the Godward path and the practice of holy virtues.

In the *Brihadaranyaka Upanishad,* it is mentioned that Yajnavalkya taught Maitreya the knowledge of the Absolute

In the *Brihadaranyaka*, there is mention of such effulgent women-sages as Gargi, and Maitreya and in the *Mahabharatha*, the names of Sulabba and Yogini are found. Women should be inspired by their moral rectitude and their steadfastness and then walk in that path; then, only does the question of reaching that height arise. Chocoda, Madalasa and other such women attained the Realization of the absolute while in the Householder stage.

Women can, by spiritual discipline, attain the unwavering, unequaled, auspicious Absolute.

Novitiates, householders, recluses, all among women, have by their pure hearts and holy conduct, attained the goal. All women should strive to acquire their qualities.

"The spiritual guide is ten times more worthy than the teacher of arts and sciences. The father is ten times worthier than the Spiritual guide, the Mother is a thousand times worthier than the Father." This is the declaration of Manu in the *Manusmrithi*. That Smrithi[1] is the binding text for all Dharma-sastras.[2] It is the very basis. See what a great honor it paid to the mother! Lakshmi, the patron of Wealth is a Female Deity. When addressing letters to women, it is customary to begin, "To..., equal to Lakshmi, in every way"... Women are entitled to universal respect. Why, Causative Appearances of Godhead like Rama and Krishna, religious teachers like Sankara, Ramanuja and Madhwa, bearers of Wisdom like Buddha, Jesus Christ and Mohammed—were they not all born of women? Their mothers were embodiments of holy glory and they gave the world sons who transformed it. Women who follow in their footsteps and lead pure consecrated lives can claim the right for the Realization of the Absolute, and no one can deny it to them.

In fact, the Self is devoid of all difference as between men and women. It is eternal, pure consciousness itself, and self-illumining. Women can reach the status of those holy women, only when they become aware of the nature of the Self.

The patron deities of education (Saraswathi), of wealth (Lakshmi) and of Wisdom (Parvathi) are all women! Therefore, it is unbelievable that women have no right to spiritual discipline, leading to merger with the Absolute and to the final emancipation from bondage.

---

1. Recollections.
2. A scripture dealing with righteousness.

Maitreya,[3] Mira,[4] Gargi,[5] Sulabha,[6] Choodala,[7] Mahadevi,[8] Andal[9] are standing examples of the mighty heroines of the spiritual adventure into the realms of God-realization.

FOR ALL LIFE ON EARTH, WOMEN ARE RESPONSIBLE

Women are proverbially too individualistic! There is a popular belief, born out of folk-experience, that three women cannot live in unison! There is a Telugu limerick, which says, "The World shivers before one woman. The Ocean will dry up if there are two! And, if there are three, O, the stars will drop down at noon!" Why is woman so characterized? Woman is extremely deficient in Sahana. By Sahana, I mean, ability to bear defeat, fortitude, forbearance, patience, quiet suffering with no thought of retaliation. That is why woman is said to be of the weaker sex. This is a pointer to the need for women developing their forbearance. You must try to put up with difference of opinion and variety of temperaments, develop understanding and sympathy. That will strengthen your ability. When we talk of women, we have the feeling that they are weak people but this is not so. They are the embodiments of the Divine Power.

---

3. A great spiritual heroine.
4. A Saint poetess who was very devoted to Lord Krishna.
5. A great scholar mentioned in the Upanishad.
6. An ascetic. She acquired several powers by austerities.
7. Consort of King Sikhadhawa who had the spirit of detachment in great measure.
8. Wife of Shiva.
9. She testifies to the highest aspiration of the human soul towards divinity.

In the *Bhagavad Gita* it is said that God resides in women with seven different types of strength while in a man, he resides only with three such aspects. Thus, in women, Divinity exists to a great extent. There is a small example for this—you should not misunderstand or misinterpret the example. For the entire country of India there is a Commander-in-chief of the armed forces, and under his control, there will be millions of soldiers. When the General walks in, all the soldiers will literally shiver. This General, who can be the cause of fear to so many people, when he comes home, he himself shivers in the presence of his wife. There is so much strength in a woman and the world is able to go on because of this strength. A woman is like a field, while man is just a seed. If we do not have a field, the seed cannot sprout. For all life on earth, woman is responsible. Great people, great saints and even great avatars have come into this world because of the help given by a woman functioning as a mother. Thus, the strength of a woman is really very sacred. The Milkmaids were such that they provided luster to the very womanhood. Whether in the matter of patience, or forbearance, or friendship, they showed exemplary conduct. It is wrong to regard this sacred path adopted by the Milkmaids as something trivial. This sacred devotion shown by the Milkmaids and by Radha should remain the ideal example for all time.

A WOMAN ALWAYS TAKES THE LEAD

It is said that while women are devoted, men are only wise. There is an inner meaning for this statement. This is why women get the right to enter the mansion where the Overself lives. The men who parade their wisdom can enter and reach only up to the feet of the Lord when He is sitting on His throne. They cannot go further. Here, we should note that in order for the strength of simple and unsophisticated devotion as against the strength of wisdom may be shown to the world, Krishna had created this situation. Whenever we want to enter any sacred gathering or a temple, a woman always takes the lead. If we look at any instance in the *Bhagavatha* or *Bharata*, we see that it is the woman who puts the man on the path of spirituality. The hearts of our women are traditionally very tender, That is why in the *Bhagavad Gita* it has been said that we should not let a woman shed tears of sorrow. In a house, where the woman is made so sad that she sheds tears of sorrow, there will never be prosperity. This has been stated in the Vedas and the Vedas have placed the aspect of motherhood on a very high pedestal. When one gets hurt one cries out, "Mother" and not "Father." Even our country is referred to as motherland. We say, worship your mother as God, worship your father—and not the other way. The mother comes first. We say Sita Rama and not Rama Sita. Similarly we say Parvathi Parameswara and not Parameswara Parvathi. In this manner all the sacred texts like *Bhagavad Gita* and the Vedas have always given a high place to a woman. That is why in a woman the Overself is found with seven types of strength and with sixteen different aspects. Because of this divine content in woman, she can take the path of spirituality with ease. In order to show to the world this exemplary behavior of women, the Milkmaids were given a prominent place. Truly, for a human being there is no property more valuable than devotion and faith. Whatever education you may have and whatever material wealth you may have, all that will be a waste if you do not have the Lord's grace.

A woman has to maintain her house. She is not only the house wife, but on her depends the glory or otherwise of the whole country. This is why we say this is our motherland.

✣✣✣✣✣✣✣✣

THE NOBLEST QUALITY OF WOMEN IS COMPASSION

This creation has three attributes. One is its feminine nature. In the word Stree, there are three letters, *Sa, Ta* and *Ra. Sa* signifies pure attribute and *Ta* signifies dull attribute. The third letter *Ra* is the symbol of the Passion attribute. For a stree, the letter *Sa* is the first letter and the pure attribute is thus the most essential. Forbearance, humility, and obedience are the three essential qualities that go with this attribute. The next important one is the Dull attribute. Fear, humbleness and shyness are qualities which are associated with this attribute. Contrary to this, we see that where the pure and dull attributes should be present, features like courage, independence and the desire to take decisions freely are appearing. These features are to be found in some women and are becoming more pronounced in the Kali Yuga. Radha said that when the qualities of courage, freedom and independence of action are beginning to be seen in women, she would not like to continue living.

Whereas for men, there is only one home, a woman has two homes. It is the duty of women to bring reputation to the houses in which they are born and to hold high the honor of the homes into which they go. But the reputations of both the houses are being brought down to some extent because of independence of action among women. Krishna: It is usual to refer to a woman as a weak person. This should not be interpreted by saying that she is always subservient to man. It should not mean that she is supreme only in the kitchen. The reputation of the entire home and even a whole nation depends on the women. However, in the background of the culture of India, women have a specific place for certain rituals and in the giving away of some ceremonial gifts and it is in this background that they are referred to as being "weak." When Harischandra was giving away his kingdom, Chandramati had a role to play. While giving away gifts, the wife also should be a party to it. Otherwise, it will not be a good gift. She is therefore given a prominent place and described as the better half. We will take another instance. When Ramachandra wanted to perform the Horse sacrifice, he could not do so, because Sita was not with him. They had to create a golden idol of Sita to satisfy the requirement of her presence. In that manner, whenever a Yagna is performed, according to tradition, the wife must also be sitting along with the husband and then only the ritual will be completed. In that context, the husband and wife are referred to as Somadeva and Somadevi respectively. Because of a situation, where such a ritual cannot be undertaken by a woman alone, she has been referred to as "weak." One cannot interpret this word by saying that a woman is weak in regard to mental or physical stamina. Women are called "weak" because they yield to anger and sorrow, much more easily than men; so I would ask them to take extra pains to overcome these two. Recital of the Name of the Lord is the best antidote for this; and if only men and women take it up, the Lord will come to their rescue. That will instill the faith that everything is God's Will and teach you that you have no right to exult or despair.

Here, in the aspect of womanhood, one must observe and draw attention to a great quality which may be described as compassion. The next quality that we must note is their ability to sacrifice. The make-up of a woman is such that she will give protection in spite of many faults. She can also be compared to an educational institution where she will teach patiently like a good teacher, even if the recipient is not willing to learn. She may also be described as a happy home where she is arranging everything without thinking of any discomfort for herself. We can also think of a woman as a person of sufficient spiritual strength by which she can make Aja, Hara, Hari or God himself play like a child before her. She can also be described as one full of sacrifice and compassion. The home of the wife is the school where the husbands can learn everything. Radha said that the sacred form of womanhood was taking a very distorted route these days.

✣✣✣✣✣✣✣✣

THE END OF FEMININITY

Women can in a unique way, deal with children lovingly, affectionately, intelligently and enthusiastically.

Women have goodness in ample measure. They are by nature helpful, tender, compassionate, humble and truthful. Next, they have also a good measure of passiveness. They are timid, shy and unenterprising. It is good that women are such. They have been endowed by nature with only a small measure of passion. Passion makes women aggressively bold, adventurous and desirous of freedom from restraint.

The day when passion is accepted as a mark of womanhood will mark the beginning of the end of femininity.

The feminine is the foundation on which a peaceful and happy world is to be raised. When woman are true and brave, kind and compassionate, virtuous and pious, the world can have an era of peace and joy.

Woman has been extolled in ancient scriptures as well as classical poetry as the Goddess of Prosperity in the home. She is the companion of the husband in the fulfillment of the duties and rights of wedded life as a householder. The woman who is attached to her husband by means of Love is indeed a flower radiating rare perfume. She is a precious gem, shedding luster in the family. A wife endowed with virtue is really a brilliant jewel. The ideal for women is the status of wife, the faithful wife and the loving mother.

✣✣✣✣✣✣✣✣

WOMAN IS THE FAITHFUL COMPANION OF MAN

Woman is considered as the Embodiment of the Goddess of Energy. She is the faithful companion of Man, his Fortune. Since she is the concretisation of the Will of the Lord, she is mystery, wonder, the representative of the protective Principle; the Queen of his home, his beneficence, the illumination of the house.

Really, woman should strive to achieve the knowledge of the Soul and live every moment in the consciousness of her being only the Self. She must evince always a desire to become one with the Divine Consciousness. The home where the woman is such and where the husband and wife are leading their lives in the shade of great ideals, where they, together sing the glory of the Name of the Lord and spend themselves in good deeds, where there reigns truth, peace and love, where regular reading is done of holy books, where the senses are under control and where there is equal treatment for all creation prompted by the knowledge of the basic unity of all creation, such a home is certainly Heaven on Earth.

A wife with such a nature is a wife worth the name. She must have real love towards the husband. Then only can she be called house-wife. Then only is she the Instrument and Companion for righteousness, wealth and desire. She who knows the mind of the husband and speaks soft and sweet is the real friend. Indeed, it is the woman who maintains the home; that is her mission. She is truly the representative of the mother of the universe.

Woman must accord first place to the service of her husband; that is True Worship, for her. Her prayers and worship and puja can wait. Without serving the husband. She cannot attain bliss in worship or meditation.

As a matter of fact, the Lord must be welcomed as represented by the husband and all service rendered to him must be elevated to the level of worship. That is the path of genuine duty. If every act is done as if it is for the sake of the Self and its merger with the Overself, then activity becomes dedicated to the Lord. All such acts save. They do not bind. She must feel, on the other hand, that the welfare of the husband, the joy of the husband, the wishes of the husband, the salvation of the husband, are the panacea for her also. Such a woman will receive the Grace of the Lord, automatically, without special effort. It will be showered upon her. The Lord will always be by her side and be kind to her in all ways. By her virtue, she will ensure the salvation of her husband. Women who are full of knowledge, who are cultured, who are bound by love and who are keen on discriminating whether their words and deeds are in conformity with righteousness—such women are like the Goddess Lakshmi, bringing joy and good fortune to the home. That home, where the husband and the wife are bound together by holy love, where every day both are engaged in the reading of books that feed the soul, where the Name of the Lord is sung and His Glory remembered, that home is really the Home of the Lord, Vaikunta!

MODESTY

MODESTY IS THE TEST OF A

WOMAN'S GRANDEUR

CHASTITY

CHASTITY IS THE CROWN JEWEL

OF WOMEN

MODESTY

Modesty is essential for woman. It is her priceless jewel. It is against Righteousness for a woman to overstep the limits of modesty; crossing the limits brings about many calamities. Why, the very glory of womanhood will be destroyed. Without modesty, woman is devoid of beauty and culture. Humility, purity of thought and manners, meekness, surrender to high ideals, sensitivity, sweetness of temper—the peculiar blend of all these qualities is modesty. It is the most invaluable of all jewels for women.

The modest woman will ever keep within limits, through her innate sense of propriety. She becomes automatically aware, which behavior is proper and which is improper. She will stick only to virtuous deeds and behavior. Modesty is the test of a woman's grandeur. If a woman has no modesty, she is injuring the interests of womanhood itself, besides undermining her own personality. She is like a fragranceless flower, which the world does not cherish or honor, or even approve. The absence of modesty makes life, for a woman, however rich in other accomplishments, a waste and a vacuum. Modesty lifts her to the heights of sublime holiness. The modest woman wields authority in the home and outside, in the community as well as in the world.

The honor and respect given to woman today is rendered by people who do not know what to appreciate and how. They do not know the standards of judgment, they have no faith in the ultimate values, they do not respect the really good and great. How can we call the thing they offer as "honor" or "respect"? It can only be called "a disease" or at best, "etiquette," that is all.

The principles of the Divine conduct will not allow the term "woman" to be applied to "a woman without modesty." If respect and honor are heaped upon a person who does not follow Divine Conduct, it is like heaping decorations on a body that has no life in it. The Soul that has left the body cannot enjoy the respect shown to the corpse. So too, if a person who is unaware of the Reality, who has not experienced the purpose of the Self's embodiment, is crowned with fame and glory, who derives joy therefrom?

The modest woman will not stoop for such meaningless trash and tinsel. She will rather seek self-respect, which is much more satisfying. That is the characteristic which makes her the Lakshmi of the Home. That is why the wife is referred to as the Goddess of prosperity in the home. If the wife has no such mark, the home becomes a seat of ugliness.

CHASTITY

Chastity is the ideal for womankind. By the strength derived from that virtue, they can achieve anything. Savithri was able, through that power, to win back the life of her husband. She actually fought with the Lord of Death.

Chastity is the crown-jewel of women. That is the virtue for which she has to be most extolled. Its beneficent consequences defy description. It is the very breath of her life. By means of her chastity and the power it grants, she can save her husband from calamity. She saves herself by her virtue and wins, without doubt, even heaven. Through her chastity Damayanthi burnt into ashes a hunter, who attempted to molest her, by the power of her "word."

EDUCATED WOMEN

THEY ARE THE PROMOTERS OF RIGHTEOUSNESS FOR THE WHOLE WORLD

VIRTUE IS THE SIGN OF THE EDUCATED WOMEN

THEY ARE ENAMORED OF THE PSEUDO-FREEDOM WHICH FEEDS THEIR CONCEIT

BABA SAYS

I do not declare that women should not be educated or that they should not move in society. Women must be given education in a well-planned manner. Unbridled freedom is destructive of Righteousness; besides, women will, by this means, harm themselves.

Women are harming themselves by running after fleeting pleasure, regardless of the need to develop good character and elevating qualities. Their mission is to lay down the canons of rightness and morality. They must provide children with moral and spiritual training.

The coming generation is shaped by the mothers of today; this generation is so full of unrighteousness and injustice, because the mothers who brought it up were not vigilant and intelligent enough.

EDUCATED WOMEN

Education is necessary for both men and women. But education for women has to be in accordance with their special needs. Educated women are really the promoters of Righteousness for the whole world. Parents too must cooperate in making them equipped with proper education. Women should not be given freedom in certain matters. I will not approve of their being given such freedom. They must be made into ideal women. Their education must be so shaped.

Unbridled freedom is destructive of Righteousness. Besides, women will, by this means, harm themselves. Mixing in society, without any discrimination will produce results that are ruinous. Of course, there were educated women in the past also, but they never gave up their righteousness. They never forgot the goal of Divine conduct. Education must be built on the basis of discrimination. Sulabha, Savithri, Anasuya, Gargi, Nalayani and other such models of chastity, devotees of the Lord like Meera, yoginis, like Chooda, all were born in India and by their adherence to Righteousness, they strengthened Righteousness. Once, when Sulabha was discoursing on the Self with all her scholarship and experience, even Janaka was astounded! It is through the example of such great and holy women with their character and conduct inspired by Devotion and Wisdom that even today simplicity, humility and devotion shine in the hearts of the women of India.

Women must ever have before her as her guide the ideal of Righteousness and progress in spiritual discipline. She can master any subject related to the objective world which has gained prominence today; but the welfare of the spirit should not be forgotten. She must get interested in Vedanthic study which cultivates the Inner Vision. A woman without this training is a rock without support, a danger to herself and others, a very unbalanced individual.

The responsibility of the elders and the parents is very great in this. Take the students of today; no trace of culture can be seen in them. Matters of the spirit and talk of the Self raise laughter among them! A mastery of words, a servitude to tailoring—these have become the fashion. This is not genuine culture. The educated women of today are helpless when it comes to managing a home. Home to them is but a hotel, they are so helplessly dependent on the cook and the maid. The educated woman is but a painted doll, decorating the modern home. She is a handicap to the husband, a weight around his neck. He is squeezed by her insistent demands for spending money on all kinds of objects. She does not share in the tasks of housekeeping and so by sheer idleness, and eating and sleeping without exercise, she develops illness which leads her quickly to death.

WOMEN ARE HARMING THEMSELVES

The wanton behavior of women has enveloped the world of today in an atmosphere of declining Righteousness. Women are harming themselves by running after fleeting pleasure, regardless of the need to develop good character and elevating qualities. They are enamored of the pseudo-freedom, which feeds their conceit. To get fixed up in a job, to earn degrees, to move about with all and sundry without distinction and discrimination, to discard respect for elders and give up fear of sin and evil, to overlook the claims of the good and the holy, to force the husband to dance to one's tune, to deny the tribute of repentance to one's errors, are these the signs of education? No; they are all the monstrous shapes of ignorance. The uneducated egoist attitudes that make a person ugly and repelling.

If the wife feels that the husband's home is sacred, then that home itself will endow her with every skill and qualification. There is no place anywhere which excels such a home for her. One saintly poet has sung that it is her temple, her school, her playground, her political arena, her field of sacrifice, her hermitage.

Educated women can do useful service to the community around them, according to their skill, taste, inclination, desire, character, educational status, mode of living, discipline or scholarship. They should avoid tarnishing the reputation of their parents, their family or themselves. A woman without a good character is as bad as "dead"; so, women must be ever vigilant when they move about in the world. They should avoid flippant talk or free mixing. The discriminating women will engage only in such acts as will add to the luster of her husband's fame and honor, never an act which will tarnish it. That is why it is said, "virtue is the sign of the educated person, the thing which makes education worthwhile."

THE CAT HOLDS THE KITTEN AS WELL AS THE RAT

I do not declare that women should not be educated or that they should not move in society. Whatever they study, wherever they move if they are endowed with good qualities, and if the good qualities are accompanied by good actions and good habits, and adherence to Ancient Wisdom and Spiritual discipline, then, their study is really worthwhile and society is indeed benefited. Study and society are not harmful in themselves. They react with the nature of the persons who make use of them and yield good or bad results. The cat holds the kitten as well as the rat in the selfsame mouth, but with what a difference! The kitten, it fondles; the rat, it kills. The bite is neutral, it is the rat or kitten that decides how it behaves.

So too, knowledge can develop discrimination, inspire the springs of service, prompt inquiry into the Reality, promote the search for the Absolute, and even pave the way for attaining Realization. On the other hand, it might feed and strengthen the roots of falsehood, hypocrisy, cruelty and injustice. It might teach man newer means of deceit and ruin the career of man on earth. It might turn Love into poisonous hatred and Truth into a bone of contention.

Therefore, whatever subject a woman might have studied and mastered, whatever the degree she has won, whatever the status of her husband or of herself, she must hold fast to these truths: Real charm consists in good character. Morality is the very breath of woman; modesty, the very live force. Adherence to truth is her daily duty. She must plant the seedlings of fear (fear of sin, fear of the Lord) in her heart and cultivate the charm of humility. In the religious, moral and physical fields, she must adhere to the strict dictates of Righteousness and take that as the essence of all education. She must be prepared to sacrifice even her life for the sake of maintaining honor. She must nourish and preserve her chastity and her adoration of the husband. This is the chief righteousness of woman. This is the reason for her very birth as Woman.

ON WHAT IS PROGRESS BASED

On what is progress based? The progress of the nation, the community and the family, depends on the proper education of women. The country can be lifted to its pristine greatness only through women mastering the science of Realization of the Reality. If the nation must have lasting prosperity and peace, women have to be trained through an educational system which emphasizes moral conduct and moral qualities. The cause for the present fall in moral standards and absence of social peace is the neglect of this aspect of women's education. The earth and sky are still the same; the change is in the ideal of education, from Righteousness to injustice.

The education of today is spoken of as Education, but that is merely a way of calling it. It does not deserve that name if you consider the present actions of the educated and their personality traits. The educated person must be capable of imbibing the inner joy of the Self, irrespective of external circumstances. He must have grasped the purpose of existence. He must be aware of the discipline of Realization. The Grace of the Lord was the Diploma which every student sought to secure in the old days. That Diploma was awarded to those who were proficient in the cultivation of morality, the knowledge of the Self, the sublimation of instincts, good conduct, pure habits, control of the senses, restraint of the mind, and the development of divine qualities. Today, however, things are different. Diplomas can now be gained by mugging up a few books! By going through modern schooling, one cannot acquire moral and spiritual training.

Women must be given education in a well-planned manner. She must be able to understand the problems of the country. She must render such service and help as she can, within the limits of her resources and capacity, to the country, the community and the family. No nation can be built except on the culture of its women. The coming generation is shaped by the mothers of today. This generation is so full of unrighteousness and injustice, because the mothers who brought it up were not vigilant and intelligent enough. Well, what is past is past. To save at least the next generation, women have to be warned in time and guided to take the ancients as their model.

Past, present or future, for all time, women are the backbone of progress, the heart of the nation, the very breath. They play the chief role in the righteousness of life here below, a key role that is charged with holiness. Her mission is to lay down the canons of rightness and morality. She must provide children with moral and spiritual training. When the mother is imbued with Righteousness, the children get the benefit and they get similarly saturated. When she is skilled in morals, the children learn to be moral. Therefore, the level of education among women decides whether a country is to prosper or decline. Her acts and conduct are critical factors.

WOMEN—OUTSTANDING POINTS

Women have proved throughout the centuries in Indian History that they have the courage, the vision and the intelligence needed to delve into the depths of spiritual silence and discipline.

Women were, all these centuries, the bulwarks of Indian culture, the guardians of Indian spiritual wealth.

It is the women who maintain the home. That is her mission.

Women have a great role to play in the moral regeneration of the people.

Women are the prop of the home and of religions.

She plants and fosters religious faith or dries up and uproots it.

It is the woman who puts the man on the path of spirituality.

Woman has been extolled in ancient scriptures as well as classical poetry as the Goddess of Prosperity.

Woman is considered as the Embodiment of Divine Energy.

She is the faithful companion of Man, his Fortune since she is the concretisation of the Will of the Lord.

She is Mystery, Wonder, the representative of the Principle; the Queen of his home, his beneficence, the illumination of the house.

Women have been its custodians and promoters; men have a secondary role.

Women have to cultivate the qualities of sacrifice and detachment, of virtue and wide vision, of integrity and honesty, of justice and righteousness so that they can lovingly transform their mates, their children into seekers and aspirants on the way to success.

Women must emerge from this College armed with deep-rooted virtue and firm faith in the ideals of womanhood, laid down in our sacred texts.

Women are taking to more education in larger and larger numbers nowadays.

Women are called weak but that is not so.

Women are the backbone of progress, the heart of the nation, the very breath.

The progress of the nation, the community and the family, depends on the proper education of women.

If the nation must have lasting propriety and peace, women have to be trained in an educational system which emphasizes moral conduct and moral qualities.

The cause for the present fall in moral standards and absence of social peace is the neglect of this aspect of women's education.

Women must be given education in a well-planned manner.

The wanton behavior of women has enveloped the world of today in an atmosphere of declining Righteousness.

Women are harming themselves by running after fleeting pleasure regardless of the need to develop good character and elevating qualities.

Woman is the faithful companion of Man.

Woman must have real love towards the husband; then only can she be called House-wife.

Sometimes, when the wife has to point out the path of Righteousness to the husband, she takes on the role even of a Father.

When the husband is down with illness she is the Mother.

Women who are the repositories of the Embodiment of Divine Energy are in no way inferior; how full of fortitude, patience and love is their nature!

Their self-control is seldom equaled by men.

They are the exemplars and leaders, for men to tread the spiritual path.

Pure selfless love is inborn in women.

They are full of fortitude and patience. Love is their nature.

The hearts of our women are traditionally very tender.

The woman who is attached to her husband by means of Love is indeed a flower radiating rare perfume.

In women, divinity exists to a great extent.

Women can take the path of spirituality with ease.

The strength of a woman is very sacred.

Chastity in the crown-jewel of women.

Chastity is the ideal for woman-kind.

Modesty in essential for woman, it is her prize jewel.

Modesty is the test of a women's grandeur.

Modesty lifts her to the heights of sublime holiness.

The noblest quality of womanhood in compassion.

Real charm consists in good character.

Morality is the very breath of woman.

Modesty the very live force.

Adherence to truth is her daily duty.

The ideal for women is the status of wife, the faithful wife and the loving mother.

The Indian ideal of marriage is that the right half is husband and the left half of the same body is the wife. Husband and wife are complementary parts of the same unit.

Remember

Great people, Great Saints and even
Great AVATARS
have come into the world because
of the help given by a woman functioning
as a Mother.
Bearers of Wisdom like Buddha, Jesus Christ
and Mohammed were they not all born
of women?
Their mothers were embodiments of Holy
Glory and they gave the world
Sons who transformed it.

MOTHER

MOTHERHOOD IS THE MOST PRECIOUS GIFT OF GOD

IT IS THE MOTHER, WHO FEEDS THE BODY AS WELL AS THE MIND

IT IS THE MOTHER WHOM THE CHILD SEES AS SOON AS IT IS BORN

BABA SAYS

How fascinating is the face of the baby, resting in the lap of the mother! It has no fear in its eyes; it has joy on its lips; it is full of peace. It is unaffected by those evil forces that rob man of his peace and joy—envy, greed, anger and hatred. It has no egoistic desire, no anxiety to impress others and show off. It has no plans for the future, no regrets for the past. Its faith in the Love and strength of the mother is so unshakable that even if the sky collapses and falls, its calmness cannot be disturbed. Why is it that, when the baby grows into adolescence and manhood, this calmness and this joy disappear, giving place to fear, anxiety and hatred. The reason is to be found in the increasing mastery of the senses and their clamor for being catered to. Again, man today tends to see only the "many." He leaves aside the vision of the One. He encounters, as a result, competition and conflict, and lives his days in sorrow, disappointment and despair.

MOTHERHOOD

MOTHERHOOD IS THE MOST PRECIOUS GIFT OF GOD

A Mother is God's nurse-maid and the duty of a mother to her children is God's Grace and this Grace is God's monthly salary to her.

It is the mother that the child sees as soon as it is born. The mother is the symbol of devotion. Love for the mother has to be fostered by everyone. He owes his food, blood and life itself to the mother. Whoever she may be, a mother is verily divine.

Maa was the first word the children uttered and the last that man gasps. She teaches the first steps for the child's unsure feet, and she sets it on the long journey towards Liberation.

India is the land that won renown in continents across the seas for heroic achievements in the material as well as spiritual fields, that swept away the mighty cohorts of her imperial conquerors, that is the nursery of famous scholars and investigators into the mysterious realms of the mind, that is upholding high traditions of music, dance, painting, sculpture and architecture that have their roots in the ancient days of adventure and achievement. This is the heritage that the sons and daughters of this country have to feed and foster. This is no weakling's task.

It requires a generation of mothers, like Kausalya who brought up Rama, Sita who fostered the charming twins Lava and Kusa. Tarabai who filled the heart of Sivaji with the earnestness and enthusiasm of epic heroes. These mothers took the children on their laps and through songs and lullabies, through gesture and good stories, while feeding and rocking them to sleep poured into the precious vessels of their hearts the nectar of the Vedas, the Upanishads and the various Yogas of India. They charged them with power and charted the road to eternal joy and peace. It is the mother, who feeds the body as well as the mind; who sings lullabies and presents pictures for the eye and the spirit; who teaches the art of pacing, of moving towards the goal of life, namely, self-realization. It gives every child knowledge of its potentialities and its limitations. It is thus the Goddess of Wealth and the Goddess of Learning, both.

Motherhood is the most precious gift of God. Love unfolds first on the lap of the mother. The eyes of love fasten themselves on the caressing face of the mother. Love then spreads towards the father, brothers, kith and kin, friend and playmate, region and language, world and its Maker. Expansion is Life. Expansion in the essence of Love. Love is God.

The baby is calm and unaffected on the lap of the mother since it has faith in the mother. The mother points to someone as its father, to another as its grandpa, to another as its sister or brother and the child accepts these statements without question. The mother creates the faith in the father for the child.

The Mother is held the object of affectionate reverence in Indian culture. She is the mistress of the house, the earliest teacher of the child, the person who lovingly transmits the culture of this ancient land to its heirs in their most formative years. The mother and the father are the first examples in social behavior that the child sees and learns to imitate. They teach adoration of God and surrender to the Highest. They represent equanimity and love before the watchful and receptive eyes of the child. So they have to be inspired to take their share in the spiritual awakening that this organization is embarking upon. Tolerance and humility have to be promoted in the rising generation through the promotion of spiritual discipline among the mothers. They are Mother Earth, which germinates the seeds and fosters them into stalwart saplings and trees. Saline soil stunts the saplings and damages the crops. Everyone has a mother as the source of his life and body. So the mother has to be strong in mind and body, ripe in culture and character, sanctified by holy thoughts and steeped in love and dedication. Good mothers make a good nation. Mothers have to be repositories of detachment, discipline and devotion. Their activity must be based on these three urges.

AS IS THE

SEED

SO IS THE

TREE

THE SEED AND THE TREE

Even if the soil is fertile, if the seed is of poor quality, it cannot grow into a good tree.

On the other hand, if the seed is good but the soil is infertile, a strong tree cannot grow. If children are to become culturally refined young persons, the parents should have the refinement of culture. When the parents observe exemplary conduct based on culture, the children will also imbibe these practices.

Today, the mothers are responsible for the good or bad behavior of their children. It is a shameful matter for the mother to say, "My son will not heed my words."

If the mother had brought up the son on right lines from the beginning, he would not behave like this. The Snake-gourd has to be made to grow straight by trying a stone to it from its tender stage. Likewise, the stone of discipline and devotion should be attached to a boy from his infancy. Mothers experience the disobedience of their children because of their failure to inculcate discipline in the early years.

This is a very appropriate story:

PUTLIBAI AND GANDHI

Gandhiji's mother, Putlibai, was a lady who believed in the two principles of truth and right conduct. She adhered to the practice of taking her morning breakfast only after hearing the first call of the cuckoo. One morning the cuckoo's call was missing for a time and Putlibai did not take her breakfast. Seeing this, the young Gandhi went to the backyard, cooed like a cuckoo and came and told his mother that she could now take her breakfast. Putlibai, who could easily guess the trick her son was playing, felt very sad about his behavior. She thought: What sin have I committed that such a son should be born to me? There is no use blaming you for what is the result of my own sin. How sinful am I that I gave birth to an untruthful son. Unable to bear her grief, she slapped the boy on the cheek and went inside.

That very moment Gandhi took a vow, "I must never again utter an untruth in my life. What is it that causes grief to a mother? In a country in which everyone is enjoined to revere the mother and father as God, I have caused grief to my mother by an act of deception." From that day he resolved only to speak the truth and never indulge in falsehood.

Mothers of those days were women of great piety and noble character. They practiced virtue and set an example to the children. Only from the wombs of such noble women were born sons of high character.

The mother of Adi Sankara, Aryaamba, was a high-souled woman, Hence, Sankara could achieve greatness and world fame. Adhering to the instructions of his mother, he led an exemplary life and achieved name and fame. Their lives shine in the pages of history as an example for mankind.

As is the seed, so is the tree.

By revering their parents and following their noble examples many great men achieved glory and fame in the past. If today we do not have high-minded youth, it is the parents that are responsible.

Today mothers who brought up such noble beings are becoming rare.

LOSES AN ESSENTIAL FERTILIZER FOR GROWTH—LOVE

The mother must know the secret of mental peace, of inner silence, of spiritual courage, of contentment which is the greatest wealth, and of spiritual discipline which gives lasting joy.

Mothers must assume this responsibility and not throw it on ayahs or on governesses. Of course, ayahs and governess are industrious and sincere. I have nothing to say against them. But the child that is brought up by the ayah loses an essential fertilizer for growth: Love. The child is denied the most health-giving vitamin: Love. The home where the fragrance of this Love has to be inhaled has now lost its sacred atmosphere. The household where the parents, brothers and sisters, kith and kin, masters and servants all lived as one "family," each familiar with the whims and fancies of the rest, respecting and loving each all the more for that knowledge is fast disappearing. There is no shrine for God in most houses. Even if there is, it is in a corner of the kitchen, where no one can sit and spend some time in meditation; or, the worship of God in that shrine is performed by a paid priest. It is an empty and enforced ritual.

When one's inner reactions and agitations are transmuted into the Divine, all that one experiences through the senses, the mind and the intellect take on the Divine luster, reveal their Divine core, and man is shaped in the mold of Love. One can be in the world but yet remain unaffected by it, provided this Vision is gained. All activity will then be for the Almighty, by His Grace and through His Will. Do not get work done though cooks, servants, ayahs and others, in the home. Women must not depend on these for the care of their children or attendance on their husbands. Earning leisure for meditation through these servants, is not a spiritual gain. Do all the household work as acts of worship for Him. That is more fruitful than hours of meditation, hours gained by entrusting this precious work to paid helpers.

The child should grow with the mother for the first five years of life. Many children do not know what the Love of the Mother is like. The mother should not hand over her responsibility during these years to someone else and be called simply "Mummy" as if she is some doll which the child likes to play with. Now, the children of the rich and "educated" parents are severely handicapped. They are deprived of the care and love of the parents. They are handed over to the care of servants and ayahs and they grow up in their company and habits and styles of thought. This is very undesirable.

You should never forget the fundamentals of Indian culture. Let children imbibe these, while on your laps. Do not hand them over to ayahs, who do not know the culture or even care for it. Let them learn the lessons of the *Ramayana*, through nursery rhymes. Let them not cram lines such as "Baa, Baa, Black Sheep" and become black sheep themselves!

To some extent, the children are shaping themselves on the lines of the conduct of their mothers. In the ancient days, the ideas and thoughts of the women were very sacred. At the time when the women were in the family way, they used to listen to many sacred stories like the story of Prahlada or of Markandeya, or Dhruva or Krishna. In these days, the situation is such that women in the family way see three cinemas a day. As a consequence, all the bad ideas contained in a cinema enter their mind and the children born are "Cinema Children" full of wrong ideas and emotions. It is very difficult to correct and reform such children. We will have to undergo a lot of trouble in this task but it is necessary for the sake of our country and of our people. In this large world, each one of you is like a tiny screw or a bolt.

Mothers are the makers of a nation's fortune or misfortune, for they shape the sinews of its soul. Those sinews are toughened by two lessons they should teach: fear of sin and fondness for virtue. Both these are based on faith in God, being the inner motivator of all. If you want to know how advanced a nation is, study the mothers. Are they free from fear and anxiety, are they full of Love towards all, are they trained in fortitude and virtue? If you like to imbibe the glory of a culture, watch the mothers, rocking the cradles, feeding, fostering, teaching and fondling the babies. As the mother, so the progress of the nation; as the mother, so the sweetness of the culture.

REAL JEWELS FOR WOMANKIND

It is indeed good that the girls of this town have now a High School. I appreciate the effort of all of you to start it. I see that the building and the equipment are quite satisfactory. I bless that the girls studying here as well as everywhere else (for, all schools are mine, whether I inaugurate them personally or not) may cultivate faith in righteousness and have sympathy towards all. India has to take up once again the role of the Teacher for the whole of humanity, and so, every boy and girl of this land has to attain unblemished character and lead a life of strict moral discipline. India is a word derived from Bhagavan and Rathah, the constant attachment to the Lord, and the word connotes a people who are dedicated to the service and uplift of the Divine in men. So, along with the schooling that you get under present conditions in such institutions, a schooling which helps some of you to earn a living and which gives all of you a certain polish and glitter, you must also undergo training in the Ancient Discipline which tames the instincts and controls the impulses and assures steadiness of character. But, these things are necessary for your own sake, not to speak of the role India has to play.

The value of character has to be emphasized here, for this is a School for Girls and traits like modesty and devotion to God are real jewels for womankind. Women preserve the traditional values of our culture and keep the nation on an even keel.

So, base all educational efforts on building up the character of the students. Then you can confidently think of raising on it the superstructure of curricula, etc. Pupils must know the secret of a happy life and of happy cooperation with other members of the community. There are duties to oneself, one's family and one's society which must be carried out intelligently and joyfully. Then only can life be harmonious and fruitful. I declare that this task of renovating and recasting education is a part of My Mission, and before long you will find Me engaged in it, and chastising those who simply talk loud and long of reconstruction and the preservation of spiritual values.

WILL BECOME MOTHERS TOMORROW

Girls are the makers of the homes of this land and so this school is a very basic institution, essential for this town. Woman is honored in this land as the Lakshmi of the Home, as the companion in the pilgrimage towards God and Self-realization, and as the mistress of the home. If the women of a country are happy, healthy and holy, the men of that country will be hardy, honest and happy. Thyagaraja has sung that even the strongest of heroes are swayed by the wishes of woman, and so, woman has a very crucial role in individual and social uplift. Therefore, I will not burden girls with the study of the geographical minutiae of America, Australia or Germany. I would rather they knew the technique of mental calm and social harmony and service and economic contentedness. Let them develop a dread of falsehood, of sliding into moral error. That is more important than even the development of the dread of God. Let them also know something of the joy that service to those in distress can give, service without a thought of the benefits that may follow from the sympathy shown. Let them learn to lay aside the egoism that poisons the service of even veterans in the field, who go about extolling themselves as founders and promoters for the service of the poor and the maimed, of this institution and that. The joy of the service is the act itself. The fruit of the seva is the removal of ego not its multiplication.

The students of this school will take up later the most glorious and the most responsible role of Motherhood. So, the teachers in schools for girls have a great big task before them, the shaping of the future history of this country, itself. The Mother is the Pillar of the Home, of Society, of the Nation and so of Humanity itself. Mothers must know the secret of mental peace, of inner silence, of spiritual courage, of contentment which is the greatest wealth, and of spiritual discipline which gives the lasting joy.

The mother should teach the children the value of the recital of the Name of God, and of mental and physical cleanliness. She should be like the mother in the story told by Vivekananda, who advises her son to call upon Krishna in the woods, while going to school alone and helpless.

The father and the mother must supplement at home the training given by the teacher at school. They must acquaint themselves with the lessons the child receives in the school and see that their conduct and advice do not conflict with what the child learns from the teacher whom it adores.

Schooling is not merely for earning a living and learning to enjoy leisure. It is to activate the Divine qualities of discrimination, renunciation and keenness of intellect to ensure in the individual the stabilizing virtues of peace, truth and righteousness through the blossoming of Love. The root is education and the fruit is virtue.

The reason which prompted the establishment of this college is: the need for women, who as mothers, will foster the expansion of love to include fellow-beings everywhere. The first step for this expansion is the home. Your love too must fill your home and your society, and finally, burst even those bonds and become worldwide. A drop of water held in the palm is soon evaporated; it is too much alone. But drop it into the sea, it survives as a part of the sea. It assumes the name and the taste, the majesty and might of the sea!

The young girls who are studying in this college today will become mothers tomorrow. It is therefore necessary that they should equip themselves with all the culture, learning and wisdom that they need in their future lives.

WHAT IS A HOME?

Indian Culture is really world culture since it can correct and channelize the human emotions and motives along healthy productive routes. It is sacred and basic and it can establish peace and joy in the hearts of all. It seeks to strike roots into life through the mothers and the children on their laps. Women have been its custodians and promoters. Men have a secondary role. Among women, you girl students who will be the leaders of women in the coming days, the examples which all women wish to emulate, must understand and practice this culture so that it may be preserved and it may flourish. The keenness to acquire education is now very evident among the daughters of the nation. So, great hope can be placed on them in this field to reconstruction. Education must be for life, not for a living. Women have proved throughout the centuries in Indian history that they have the courage, the vision, and the intelligence needed to delve into the depths of spiritual science and discipline.

Woman has been extolled in ancient scriptures as well as classical poetry as the Goddess of Prosperity in the home. She is the companion of the husband in the fulfillment of the duties and rights for wedded life as a householder. While learning home science, you may be getting trained in the art of making the home happy and full of harmony and health. You have to learn also how to steer clear of hatred, malice, greed, anger, anxiety, pride and other obstacles that come in the way of inner peace. It its not enough if the home budget is balanced. The wife and the mother must learn the art of having a balanced view of life, which will not be affected by triumphs and troubles, gains or losses, victory or defeat. This balance can be got only by reliance on God, faith in the In-dwelling God.

One discipline you must heed is the control of the senses. If you give them free rein, they will drag you into calamity. Education must render you monarch of your talents, your tools for acquiring knowledge. The eye, the ear, the tongue are like wild horses that have no bit between the teeth. Learn the art of meditation by which the senses can be controlled and the will directed inwards, towards the mastery of feelings and emotions.

You are mastering what is called Home Science, but what is a home? How is it different from a house? The home is filled with love, with the sacrifice that love involves, the joy that love radiates and the peace that love imparts. The brick and mortar structure where parents and children spend their lives is not a home. Children do not yearn for it. Parents do not find peace therein! Many educated women have converted the home into a hotel, what with the cook, the maid, the servants, the ayah, the bearer and the chauffeur who clutter the whole place! She is just a scintillating doll, darting in and through the rooms. She is often a millstone round the neck of the husband, whom she leads about and lords over, to his utter discomfiture. She engages herself in spending money, shopping for things of her wayward fancy. In order to keep up social appearances, she idles away the time in lazy lounging and medicating herself for imaginary illness. She becomes a burden on her spouse and children.

The center of every home must be the shrine room. The fragrance of flower and incense emanating from there must pervade the home and purify it. The mother must set the example in holding out the shrine, as the heart of the household. She must enforce discipline over the children in personal cleanliness, in humility and hospitality, in good manners and acts of service. She must persuade the children, by example and precept, to revere elders and spend some time both in the mornings and evenings for prayer, and for silent meditation. The shrine room has to be kept clean and consecrated. Special festival days, marked out in each religion, should be observed, so that the significance will impress itself on the young minds. However self-centered and haughty the husband is, by systematic regulation of the domestic timetable, with worship of God as its focal point, the man can be made to realise how a God-centered home is a home of peace and joy. He too will soon fall in and be a pillar of faith.

ONLY THE WIFE NOT THE MOTHER

The mother herself must take charge of the education of children during the early years. If the children are handed over to servants and ayahs, they will learn their habits of living and speech, and they will weep only when they die, not when the mother dies! For, they start loving the ayah more than the mother, who has shoved it onto another, as a nuisance and a bother! She must herself prepare food for the home. For, food which is prepared with love and served with a smile, is much more sustaining and strengthening, than food cooked by a hired woman and served by a disgruntled, refractory kitchen boy!

I am glad cookery and nutrition are included in your syllabus. I smell, even here, while on the dais, some dishes being got really in your culinary laboratory! Your knowledge of cookery reaches far, I must admit! The constituents of a tasty dish attract the senses and titillate them, no doubt. But, I hope you learn also about the distinctions between the pure and passionate and dull types of food and of the effect of these on character. The mind is the key to health and happiness and so food must be so chosen that it does not affect the mind adversely. Along with pure, balanced food, the mind must also be given a special diet of meditation, prayer beads, repetition of the name of God, etc. to keep it sound and steady.

The status of the mother in the home is one of authority. Now, even colleges like this, try to train up only the wife, not the mother. The home for which science caters here is the home where the wife rules, not where the mother spreads her affection, and shapes the future of the country and its culture! Let the children, even grown-up boys and girls, touch the feet of the father and mother every morning, before the daily tasks are started. It will generate a reverential atmosphere in the home. Five minutes in the shrine room, and the homage of prostration for parents—let this be the daily routine.

Establish the status of the mother in the home, as the upholder of spiritual ideals and, therefore, the Guru of the children. Every mother must share in this effort—the expansion and steady manifestation of the God-consciousness latent in every child.

The home is the temple where the family, each member of which is a moving temple, is nurtured and nourished. The mother is the high priestess of this House of God. Humility is the incense with which the house is filled. Reverence is the lamp that is lit, with love as the oil and faith as the wick. Spend the years of your lives dedicating them for such worship, in the homes that you will found. I bless you so that through your faith and strength, devotion and dedication may increase in this land. Let the home be harmonious, happy, smooth running, with no friction or faction. Let the various individuals comprising the home, the different generations and levels of intelligence, growth and attainments living together, let all learn to live together, with understanding and sympathy, fortitude and forbearance, in mutual cooperation and loving-kindness. Let peace reign in your homes, between the mother and her children, the brothers and sisters, the kith and kin.

Make the home a seat of harmony. Then the village will be a home for concord. The state will be having peace, the nation will be happy and the world will have prosperity.

WHEN WOMEN RUN AFTER JOBS WHO IS TO RUN AFTER THE FAMILY?

Degrees and diplomas have become worthwhile because they entitle you to a job. They are begging bowls, with which you can clamor outside the doors of offices and factories.

A college education gives you the chance to earn a few rupees and live thereupon. But unless it destroys certain illusions that are nourished by the common level of mankind, your lives will not be happy. One illusion which is basically undesirable is: living under the impression that you are the body and that you are destroyed with the death of the body. Another illusion is: happiness consists in accumulating money or knowledge or comforts or reputation. Trying to be happy through such accumulation is like getting into the Madras Bus and hoping to reach Bangalore. What is happiness? It is the state of mind, which is unaffected by fortune, good or bad. That is a state of mind, different from the state of status or storing objects or things. By systematic education, the mind can attain that state. This can be done without reducing man into an inert, dull, useless individual. If activity is done as worship, then, the mind will be steady and free from anxiety.

Srimathi Giri said that the misery of some unemployed women is more pitiable than that of their brothers. This situation has arisen because the real significance of education has been missed by educators, educated, and educatees! Education must strengthen the springs of Bliss, Love and Peace that are inherent in the heart. These should not be dried in the dusty years of study. Man is in essence a fountain of eternal joy, peace, love and devotion. Cultivate these, by precept and example and exercise, during the formative years. Then, the educated will have security and sweetness as long as they live.

Of course livelihood has to be earned; but when, as happens now, both husband and wife work in an office away from home, children grow on the laps of ayahs and the shoulders of servants, learning their language and manners. The father and mother become casual strangers. When the food they eat is not prepared by loving hands and served with affectionate smiles, the savor disappears and the vibrations are often vile. The mother, as a teacher, attends school leaving off her natural role as the teacher of her own children! This is indeed a tragedy! The house where such parents live can never become the home that children love to cherish in memory.

Women are taking to modern education in larger numbers nowadays. They are serving in offices, schools and factories. They are also rising to positions of authority in other fields. But most of them are prompted by urges of personal aggrandizement rather than ideals of service. They desire more and more material comforts. But when women run after jobs, who is to run the family? If both father and mother move into offices to earn money, what becomes of the children? Pouring over books, how can the kitchen work? More money may be earned, but it leads only to more anxiety, more unrest and more loss. The women who take up jobs are finding that they have no happiness worth the name. The educated women must utilize her knowledge and skill to bring up her children into healthy, virtuous and disciplined patriots, so that they may be of great use to the country, the culture and the community. Earning money is not the end-all of education. It is the greed to earn money by any means, as fast as possible that has led to the evils that we see in society today. Money breeds pride, fosters hatred.

THEN ONLY CAN THEY AS MOTHERS

Women must emerge from this College armed with deep-rooted virtue and firm faith in the ideals of womanhood laid down in our sacred texts. Then only can they, as mothers, mold their children as bright, beautiful, valorous, strong citizens of the world. This is the only way out of the horror in which the world is simmering.

Now, the education that is being given in schools for girls and in women's colleges help only to make them "desirable wives," not "desirable mothers." The role of the mother which is the natural, native and inescapable role is neglected; the subsidiary short-lived scintillation is given prominence.

The securing of jobs cannot be allowed to overshadow the real purpose of education. Women have to cultivate the qualities of sacrifice and detachment, of virtue and wide vision, of integrity and honesty, of justice and righteousness so that they can lovingly transform their mates and children into seekers and aspirants, on the way to success. There are many women present here. So, I must tell them this: though they have faith and devotion, they promote anxiety by their attitudes and behavior. They have a great responsibility which they have neglected. Anxiety and worry are growing in the family and in society due to their neglecting the discipline that trains people to live self-controlled lives. They do not distinguish between a cinema hall, a market or an exhibition, but talk and chatter everywhere, even in a temple, or a holy gathering. Children learn from them and they too, when they grow up, lose all reverence for elders and holy places. They talk loud and long and very irreverently, and add to the anxiety, and restlessness instead of reducing it.

BABA SAYS

Parents must feel that they are servants appointed by the Lord to tend the little souls that are born in their households, as the gardener tends the trees in the garden of the Master.

PARENTS SET BAD EXAMPLES

I am glad I came here and met these children. 1 am glad that their parents, especially, their mothers have also been invited and are present. For they should know the school which their children attend and the teachers who train them, so that they may contribute their gratitude to those who share their responsibility.

More than all, the character of the children must be made strong and pure. Give them all the confidence and courage they need to become good, honest, self-reliant children. It is not enough if they learn something by which they can make a living. The manner of living is more important than the standard of living. The children must also have reverence towards their religion, their culture, their educational attainments and their country. They must learn well their mother tongue, so that they can appreciate the great poetical works and epics written by the seers of their land. This will give them valuable guidance in the stormy days ahead. They must also develop a deep reverence for their motherland, for India is the most ancient as well as the wisest teacher of humanity and every child born here has a great responsibility to know, respect and practice the teaching which is so universal and so meaningful.

The human heart when young is very soft. It responds to grief and pain in fellowmen. It is the example of elders, the lessons they receive from parents and the company they get into, the training they get in school and society that harden these hearts into stone. Keep those hearts soft. Learn to share with others their grief and their joy. Do not act jealous when others are happier or when others win prizes or credits in examinations. Emulate their industry, pray for a higher share of intelligence or a sharper memory. Do not give room in your hearts to envy and malice. Envy is deadly poison. It will contaminate character, ruin health and rob you of peace. Be unaffected by envy and you can subdue the Gods of Creation, Protection and Destruction. Like a pest that destroys growing crops, envy enters slyly and spreads quickly. So even in small matters you must be vigilant that you do not become envious. Parents also must not find fault with others in the hearing of children, or show their hatred or envy of others before these tender minds.

The hearts of children are pure, they are drawn easily and naturally to the Feet of the Lord, for they have no attachment to sensory objects preventing them from inhaling aright the fragrance of the Divine Glory. The Bliss that radiates from the faces of these children is evidence of their innate simplicity and sweetness.

The parents themselves are not competent to guide the children. They dote on them and do not know how to correct them. They have reprehensible habits and ways of life. They smoke, play cards, gamble, drink and fight in the home. They utter falsehoods, talk scandal, boast and slander, in the presence of the children. How then can they lead their children on right lines? You will have to persuade such parents to mend their ways and be inspiring examples, rather than enemies and obstacles.

Parents talk of honesty but they utter lies in the presence of children and even encourage them to speak falsehood. The father, while at home, asks the child to tell the unwelcome visitor that he is not at home! The child is thus taught his first lesson in prevarication by the father himself. There is no use blaming him if he grows into a social menace.

LET ME TELL YOU A STORY

I must give the elders, the parents who are here in large numbers, some advice. Do not set bad examples for these children to follow. If you are truthful, just be calm under provocation and full of love in all your dealings with others, these children too will grow up in Truth and Righteousness, Peace and Love. If you tell your son, when you are actually at home, and someone is calling on the telephone, to reply that you are not at home you are sowing a poisonous seed which will become a huge tree. Let me tell you a story to illustrate the danger of such small beginnings. A mother carried her son on her shoulder when she went to the market. A woman with a basket of fruits passed by her. The child lifted a banana from the basket and started eating it. The mother noticed it and when she was told that he had cleverly lifted it from the basket of a passing fruit-seller, she complimented the son on his smartness. This made the child indulge in petty thieving and picking pockets as he grew into a boy and in actual house breaking and dacoity. Once during a dacoity, he even committed murder, and when he was caught and jailed, he expressed a wish to see his mother before being hanged. The wailing, weeping, desperate mother was brought before him. She was sobbing at her son's fate. The son asked her to come closer to him. Suddenly he tried to strangle her and the guards separated them. The son said, "she deserves the punishment. For, it was she who brought me to this doom. Had she reprimanded me when I stole a banana when I was a child of two years, instead of complimenting me, I would not have fallen into this evil way."

Parents set bad examples—uttering falsehood, scandalizing others, gambling, drinking, behaving violently, inflicting injury, becoming addicted to nightclubs, pictures and drinking parties, quarreling at home after arriving home past midnight. How can children, used to such low sights and sounds, learn to become bright, fresh, fragrant flowers of the ancient Garden of India ?

CHILDREN MUST MAKE THE ELDERS ASHAMED

Indian traditions and Indian modes of living are now being fast cast away. Crude manners of dress and speech and personal appearance are replacing them. Children should be taught to look upon these with disgust. They should know them for what they are: aberrations and vulgarities! Now, obscene posters are pasted along the roads by cinema theaters in order to attract fans. They contaminate character very subtly and silently. Children must make the elders ashamed when they permit such demeaning and deleterious posters to appear in public view! They have to waken the elders into a sense of shame, at the lowering of human values. Unless we plant these ideals in the children, India will go down to the depths of degradation.

How can you tolerate these obscene pictures, these posters publicizing pornographic films, this most objectionable type of dress, this brazen behavior and appearance? Do everything possible to root out this evil. Train the children and the young to remove this blot from the face of the earth.

When the mind in turned towards God or goodness it become human. If it is turned towards evil thoughts and wicked egoism it becomes demoniac.

If a man wishes to be happy and healthy, the first exercise he must do is to remove from his mind every bad thought, feeling and habit. What is the next step? He must welcome good thoughts, good feelings and good habits. These exercises can be started even from childhood. Removing the bad and substituting it with the good has to be done by you as a teacher for your pupil. You must be vigilant to prevent the children from being spoiled by the evils of injustice, violence, immorality and falsehood. This is the austerities imposed on you as your duty.

The parents themselves are not competent to guide the children. They dote on them and do not know how to correct them. They have reprehensible habits and ways of life. Instill love and harmony in the tender minds of boys and girls. They are now lovely creepers who depend on you and your care for their proper growth and blossoming.

PARENTS' FAULT

It is an unfortunate fact that today ninety percent of the children are spoiled by the parents themselves. The parents do not exercise timely control over the children. If the wrong actions of the children are corrected then and there, they will grow in the proper way. The parents should show no indulgence towards children who go astray. It is misplaced affection to let erring children go uncorrected.

What use is there in having children who do not behave properly? There is no meaning in rejoicing when a child is born. The time for rejoicing will come when the child grows up, earns name and fame and brings credit to the parents.

Every son should see that he makes his mother happy. He should seek from the mother nothing but her love and blessings. Mothers should strive to keep their children on the straight path. Only such mothers and children are worthy of the name. When mothers and children act properly, the nation will develop along right lines. Righteousness will spread from the family to the whole world.

There are parents who question their children when they go to Swami: "What madness has seized you? Why are you going to that Sai?" What form of madness do these parents desire for their progeny? Do they want them to become rowdies and goondas? Do they want them to be crazy about money. What will money give them which can equal the grace of God? What everyone should seek is the grace of the Divine which is a treasure greater than all the wealth in the world.

✣✣✣✣✣✣✣✣

DISCIPLINE MUST BE TAUGHT

There is also another responsibility that devolves upon the parent. As laid down in the Scriptures, he must live the householder's life of righteous conduct so that a picture of a pure, happy life may be imprinted on the young mind. If the parent is a drunkard, a gambler and a cheat, no amount of textbook ethics can cure the son. I will not allow them to be blamed. Discipline must be taught. They must develop proper outlook. They must cultivate clean, healthy habits. They must learn thrift and the proper use of money. When children. learn how to use money with care and without waste, the future will be bright. Children must also learn and practice good manners at home and outside, and follow good norms of behavior.

I like children and the young and the innocent. I will not allow then to be blamed.

The fault lies wholly on the shoulders of the elders, the parents, the leaders who shape the norm which they imbibe. Teach them the lessons of love, sacrifice and contentment.

The older persons have but a little distance to travel, before they disembark. But the children remember, have many miles to go and they take the nation along with them to perdition or progress! The sages of old knew the value of our culture and the deep peace and security that the heritage of that culture can give in these days of turmoil and strife. So they prescribed three disciplines for everyone, young or old. They declared: worship your mother as God, worship your father as God, worship your teacher as God. So long as a nation grows up with these three ideals, it can never be pulled up by its roots and get dried up.

For, adoration of the mother as Divine, of the father as God and of the Preceptor as God will make the growing generation cherish the heritage, which is handed down by them and through them. The generation gap will not be an unbridgeable chasm.

✣✣✣✣✣✣✣✣

TRAIN THE MINDS OF THE YOUNG IN THE GLORY OF GOD

Let the mind dwell ever on God. Let it see all as God. That is what is described as one-pointedness. If it is so fixed, it will give up its tendency to search for faults and foibles in others. It will not run after the foul and the frivolous. It will not accumulate the trivial and the transitory. The body is as the container of the torch. The senses are the bulb. The mind is the cell, but, have intelligence as the switch. Then, it will not be turned towards the undesirable. It will be used only to help man's progress towards Divine Destiny. I wish to emphasize that great care is to be taken to keep the mind of the student free from blemish. The mind is like a camera. When the lens is turned against any object and clicked, the picture of that thing gets printed on the slide. So, be ever vigilant. Turn it always against the holiest of objects, God, and click. When the holy Ganga is near, why wallow in the cesspool? Contemplate on God in any form, and stay pure. Merge yourself with the whole of Creation. Allow the whole of creation to enter the portals of your mind in one happy joyful family reunion. Envy, which like a mistletoe saps vitality out of all Spiritual discipline, creeps in only when you feel your neighbor as different, distinct, disturbing. You do not feel your hand as a nuisance, because it is yours, a part of you. Your neighbor is also as much you. All men are lamps lit from the same flame which is God. From one tiny seed, the giant banyan tree, bearing billions of tiny seeds, is born. God alone knows the secret of His mighty Majesty. Out of the one seed called Creation, all this Universe has emanated, with each country as its branches and each individual as one single seed. That is why it is said that God resides in the region of the heart in all beings. The seed is hard inside the fruit. When the fruit gets rotten, the seed does not rot. The Self is unaffected by changes in the complexion of the body. Man has come with a definite allotment of time to engage himself in activities which will award him Liberation and merge him in the Universal, of which he is a drop. Remember this mission.

In homes and schools, training of the minds of the young on these lines has to be taken up earnestly by teachers and parents. Of course, they must equip themselves for this work by steady practice in meditation and recital of the Name of God. In every home, a certain length of time must be fixed every day, in the morning as well as evening, for readings from spiritual books and recital of the Name of God. Parents and children must join in singing the glory of God. In fact, all one's time must be dedicated just to God. So as the first step, a few minutes may be devoted to the adoration of His Glory or the gauging of the depth of that Glory. Gradually, when the sweetness of the habit heartens you, you will devote more and more time and feel more and more content. The purpose of "living" is to achieve the "living in God." Everyone is entitled to that consecration and consummation. You are the Truth. Do not lose faith. Do not belittle yourselves. You are Divine—however often you slide from humanity to animality or even lower.

God is everywhere. He is everything. So, it appears as if He is nowhere, and He is not in anything! For to know Him you have to identify Him as someone foreign and something unique. We forget that everything is foreign to us, everything has a uniqueness of its own! On what authority can you deny? On what authority do you accept? You cannot deny Love or

Truth or Wisdom. He is Love, Power, Truth, Wisdom, Beauty. When you accept Love, you accept God. The tender plant of spirituality can grow only in the field of Love. It cannot thrive in the dehydrated loveless land of human hearts.

Remove all traces of salinity from your hearts, adding to the soil the precious complement of the Name of the Lord. Water it with Faith. Then plant the seedlings of Divinity. Have discipline as the fence, and steadfastness as the pesticide to be sprayed. Then, you can reap the rich harvest of Wisdom which will free you from the task of cultivation forever. Those who laugh at people singing the Name of God or visiting Temples or attending Divine Discourses have not tasted the nectar, and therefore are prejudiced against it. Pity them, for they do not know what they miss.

FROM THE MOTHER TO LIBERATION

When it rains on sand, the water seeps down.
When it rains on red earth, the water stays.
When the rain falls on an oyster, a pearl is born.
Likewise devotion grows according to one's worthiness.

Embodiments of the Divine,

We hear in common parlance the terms mother, father, preceptor and God being used in that order. This has a significance of its own. It is the mother that the child sees as soon as it is born. The mother shows the child to the father. The father leads him to the preceptor and the preceptor leads him to God. Everyone should understand the inner significance of the four terms.

We hear from spiritual aspirants the four terms: Devotion, Wisdom, Renunciation and Reality in the same order. There is a significance in the order in which those terms are mentioned. Devotion awakens wisdom, wisdom promotes renunciation, and renunciation confers the knowledge of Reality. We can reach the mansion of liberation if we walk on the stepping stones of devotion, wisdom, renunciation and the knowledge of Reality.

The *Bhagavatham* in its very title testifies to this truth. The term Bhagavathamu in Telugu is made up of five letters: *Bha, ga, va, ta, mu*. Here *Bha* signifies devotion, *ga* signifies wisdom, *va* signifies renunciation, *ta* signifies the knowledge of Reality and *mu* signifies Liberation. The *Bhagavatha* bestows on us liberation by leading us through Devotion to Wisdom, Renunciation and knowledge of Reality.

"WHO AM I" - "I AM HE"
"KO-HAM" - "SO-HAM"

Prahlada has given us a mantra: It means that the highest intelligence consists in finding the way. What is the way to be sought? It is the way to Divinity. How is it to be found? It is by knowing the source from which you have come. Where have you come from? You have come from the Divine and you have to go back to the Divine.

From the moment of birth, man is concerned about his future. The child's first cry is, "Kwa, Kwa." "Wherefrom have I come?" If you examine what is happening to you every day, you will understand why the child cries at the time of birth. Seeing the endless troubles in store, the child cries: "Where am I?" Forgetting the place from which they came, men lose themselves in worldly desires. There are a few like Prahlada who from the moment of birth realize their inherent divinity. They utter "So-ham, So-ham!" from the time of birth. But ordinary mortals ask, "Ko-ham, Ko-ham," "Who am I?" They do not get the answer till the end of their lives. They do not realise that the answer is: "I am God." A few earnest seekers start with, "Who am I?" and end with the discovery that "I am He."

GOD—ABOVE ALL

Nothing should come in the way of your seeking God. You must be prepared for any sacrifice or face any opposition for the sake of God. Prahlada faced the wrath and hatred of his father. If a mother stands in the way of your devotion to God, you must be prepared to give her up, as Bharata did when Kaikeyi sought to separate him from Rama. Mira was prepared to renounce her husband rather than give up her devotion to Krishna.

These are examples of devotees who did not flinch from any sacrifice in vindicating their devotion to God.

The main message of the *Bhagavatha.* is devotion. The mother is the symbol for devotion. Father is the symbol for wisdom. The preceptor is the symbol for renunciation. God is the very embodiment of knowledge. We can reach the mansion of Liberation only by ascending the four steps to Divinity.

ONE'S OWN MOTHER IS

"Recognizing one's mother as the very embodiment of all Divine forces, one must show reverence to her with love. This is the true message that the Navarathri festival gives us," observed Bhagavan Baba, inaugurating on October 14th in the Poornachandra Auditorium.

Adoring one's Mother as the embodiment of Divinity:

Everyone should consider it his foremost duty today to revere the mother as divine and serve her, regardless of country or circumstance. If a man cannot respect and serve the mother, who has borne him for nine months, brought him forth into the world and reared him over the years, who else is he likely to respect? Maternal love is akin to that of the Creator who projects and protects this infinite cosmos in countless ways.

The life of a man who cannot respect and love such a venerable mother, is utterly useless. Recognizing one's mother as the very embodiment of all divine forces, one must show reverence to her and treat her with love. This is the true message that the Navarathri festival gives us. The supreme Power manifests herself in the form of Durga, Lakshmi, and Saraswati. The Navaratri festival is celebrated in order to proclaim to the world the power of these goddesses. One's own mother is a combination of all these Divine beings. She provides us energy, wealth, and intelligence." She constantly desires our advancement in life. So she represents all the three goddesses that we worshipped during the Navaratri festival.

There is no need to propitiate Durga, Lakshmi and Saraswati for material prosperity, energy and worldly knowledge. If we love and adore the mother, we shall be showing our love and devotion to all the goddesses.

Likewise, a man should show equal regard and reverence for the mothers of others as he shows for his own mother.

THE FIRST PLACE IS GIVEN TO THE MOTHER

Even in the ancient teachings about the persons who are to be revered as Gods—mother, father, teacher and guest—the first place is given to the mother, when it says, "Worship your mother as God." Even in our casual talk we say, mother, father, teacher and God. God is relegated to the last position, but the mother is given the first place. This reveals the attitude of Indian culture towards women in general and the mother in particular.

It is the mother that holds the child with her hand and teaches it how to walk. It is the mother that feeds the child and teaches it how to eat. It is again the mother who teaches the child to utter meaningful sounds and to speak. Thus the mother is one's foremost teacher. Veman observed that a son who does not care for his parents is no better than the worms that are born and die in an ant-hill.

We should deem our parents as Iswara (Great Lord) and Parvathi (Mother of the Universe) and serve them wholeheartedly. If we cannot please them, how can we hope to please God?

MOTHER'S DAY

Is a day appointed for the honoring of motherhood and the loving remembrance of one's mother.

Worship your mother as God and worship your father as God. Your worship deserves to be preserved in the casket of your hearts like precious gems.

The story of Pundarika must be added here: Pundarika was an ideal son who spent all his time in the service of his parents. Today when the mother is laid up with high fever, the son, not caring for the condition of the mother, runs to the film show.

Mother is the Goddess who has given us this blood, this body and this individuality and therefore she deserves all consideration and worship. By disregarding the mother, we shall never be able to prosper in life and we shall never be able to become good in life.

When Pundarika was serving his mother, Panduranga came there. Pundarika was pressing the feet of his mother and did not care to look at Panduranga. In the meantime Tukaram, his Guru, also came there. Tukaram asked, "My dear Pundarika, do you know who has come? It is God Panduranga! You are not caring for Him. How is it?

Then Pundarika replied, "The culture of Two Gods is not important for me but the culture of ONE GOD is important for me".

Tukaram said, "He is God."

Then Pundarika said, "Yes, He is God. This is also God."

The real God for me is my parent and not Panduranga. From the moment of my birth, I have been seeing this form and this form of my mother was responsible for the birth, growth, nourishment and sustenance of my body. Therefore, I worship her. The Goddess who has been right in front of me for the last eighteen years is more important than the God who appears for a few moments and vanishes. If Panduranga cares to grant me Darshan, let Him wait until I complete the service of my mother."

So saying, he threw a brick as a sort of seat for Panduranga to sit and wait. Even God Panduranga waited until Pundarika completed the service of his mother and then granted Darshan to him.

Even God would wait for you. Do not think that He would go away, but you must discharge your duty to the best of your ability and to your utmost satisfaction.

Pundarika was not guilty of sacrilege; for he was actually worshipping God, in His most accessible Form, the Mother.

ONE'S MOTHER IS GREATER THAN HEAVEN ITSELF

One's mother is greater than heaven itself. Sri Rama himself declared that one's mother and Motherland are greater than even heaven. The Navarathri festival teaches this profound truth. One must remember that reverence to one's own mother is one's paramount duty. Maa was the first word the children uttered and the last that man gasps. She teaches the first steps for the child's unsure feet, and she sets it on the long journey towards liberation. It is the mother who feeds the body as well as the mind; who sings lullabies and presents precious pictures for the eye and the spirit and teaches the art of pacing of moving towards the goal of life namely self-realization.

✣ ✣ ✣ ✣ ✣ ✣ ✣ ✣

MOTHERS

The child should grow with the mother for the first five years of life.

When it is five years old, the father has to take up the task of bringing it up.

Then, it must be entrusted to a Guru.

The mother and the father are the first examples in social behavior that the child sees before it and learns to imitate.

The mother teaches the first step for the child's unsure feet, and she sets it on the long journey towards Liberation.

Mothers must assume the responsibility and not throw it on ayahs or governesses.

The mother is held the mistress of the house, the earliest teacher of the child, the person who lovingly transmits the culture of this ancient land to its heirs in their most formative years.

The mother herself must take charge of the education of children during the early years.

When the mother is skilled in morals, the children learn to be moral.

The home is the temple where the family, each member of which is a moving temple, is nurtured and nourished.

The mother is the high priestess of the House of God.

She must enforce discipline over the children in personal cleanliness, in humility and hospitality, in good manners and act of service.

The character of the children must be made strong and pure.

Give them all the confidence and courage they need to become good, honest, self-reliant children.

The mother should know the school which their children attend and the teacher who trains them.

The children must revere their parents. That is their duty.

The children must also have reverence towards their religion, their culture, their educational attainment and their country.

The Mother must know the secret of mental peace, of inner silence, of spiritual courage, of contentment which is the greatest wealth, and of spiritual discipline which gives the lasting joy.

But the child that is brought up by ayah loses an essential fertilizer for growth: Love.

The child is denied the most health-giving vitamin: Love.

The mother creates the faith in the father for the child.

The mother points out to the child someone who is its father, to another as its grandpa, to another as its sister or brother and the child accepts these statements without question.

Love unfolds first on the lap of the mother. The eyes of love fasten themselves of the caressing face of the mother. It spreads towards the father, brothers and sisters, kith and kin, friends and playmates, region and language, world and its Maker.

The earlier years of the life are the most crucial and so the mother and father have to share responsibility for the proper upbringing.

Parents should not allow children to fall away from their control and wander about without compass or anchor.

They should not also spoil them by allowing them too much freedom and catering to their fancies.

Don't allow the virus of vice to infect their brains.

The parents themselves are not competent to guide the children. They dote on them and do not know how to correct them, their reprehensible habits and ways of life.

They smoke, play cards, gamble, drink and fight in the home.

They utter falsehoods, talk scandal, boast and slander, in the presence of the children.

How then can they lead their children on the right lines?

Such parents should mend their way and be inspiring examples, rather than enemies and obstacles.

If you tell your son, when you are actually at home, and someone is calling on the telephone, to reply that you are not at home, you are sowing a poisonous seed which will become a huge tree.

Parents set a bad example uttering falsehood, scandalizing others, gambling, drinking, behaving violently, inflicting injury, becoming addicted to nightclubs, arriving home past midnight.

How can children used to such low sights and sounds learn to become bright fresh fragrant flowers of the ancient Garden of India?

Parent also must not find fault with others in the hearing of children, or show their hatred or envy of others before the tender minds.

They talk loud and long and very irreverently, and add to the anxiety, and restlessness instead of reducing it.

Parent take them to films regardless of the impression they create on their tender minds,

There are many parents, who, by their behavior and habits, in full view of the children, drink, gamble and utter blatant lies, thus poisoning the tender minds of their progeny.

When the father requests the son to tell a caller at the door that he is not at home, the seed of dishonesty is planted.

Parents have to bring up their children as bright and willing citizen capable of earning their own food and helping others in distress.

Parents have to be imbued with faith in the basic truths of this Universal Religion.

The virtues you implant in them, the examples you place before them will remain carved in their memories and transform their outlook and behavior in the days to come.

The Guru sows the seeds

CHILDREN

*Children are lamps which can
illumine the path of the nation.*

*The bliss that radiate from the faces
of children is evidence of their innate
simplicity and sweetness.*

*A child's smile is sunlight in a grief-
stricken home.*

BABA SAYS

The hearts of children are pure. They are drawn naturally to the Feet of the Lord, for they have no attachment to sensory objects preventing them from imbibing aright the fragrance of the Divine Glory.

I like children and the young and innocents.
I pay them great attention.

CHILDREN ARE CHARMING SAPLINGS

The spacious mansion, called Sanathana Dharma (Ancient Wisdom) was erected by the sages of the past to provide peaceful and prosperous lives for succeeding generations. But through the neglect of the very beneficiary, it has become deserted and is being condemned as uninhabitable! The peace and joy which those sages hoped for the sons and daughters of India have disappeared from their faces. They are today visible only in the faces of these little children before me, learning in this school, as well as children elsewhere. When they grow up, the joy is turned into grief and the peace melts away into anxiety. The elders have lost the art of regaining joy and peace, and retaining them.

These children are charming saplings, full of promise, who can be made, by wise care and well-directed love, to blossom into ideal citizens, able to understand, appreciate and practice the tough discipline laid down in the Ancient Wisdom, for attaining self-knowledge, and knowledge of the Universe, which is only another aspect of the Self. The earlier years of life are the most crucial and so, the mother and the father have to share the responsibility for the proper upbringing. The skills, the attitude, the prejudices, the emotions that make or mar the future are all built into the foundation of character, during those crucial years. The parents must lay the foundation strong and straight. But what equipment have the parents now, for this task? They have no deep knowledge of their own culture. They have no faith in its values. They practice no spiritual discipline. They have no mental peace. Children must grow up in the atmosphere of reverence, devotion, mutual service and cooperation. They must be taught respect for parents, teachers and elders. Now, they learn only copybook maxims, devoid of any sincere urge to put them into practice.

Even as children, they must know the amazing handiwork of God, the most amazing, being themselves. They can well understand that they are not merely a bundle of two hands and two feet, head and stomach. They can picture a Force within them, which directs all their acts. Through singing the glory of God and through listening to stories and scriptural texts about God, these elevating truths can be instilled in them by teachers and parents.

Learn the A B C D of your own alphabet; then, you will be able to guide your children in the study of the alphabet of their lives.

More than all, the character of the children must be made strong and pure. Give them all the confidence and courage they need to become good, honest, self-reliant children. It is not enough if they learn something by which they can make a living. The manner of living is more important than the standard of living. The children must also have reverence towards their religion, their culture, their educational attainments and their country. They must learn well their mother tongue, so that they can appreciate the great poetical works and epics written by the seers of their land. This will give them valuable guidance in the stormy days ahead. They must also develop a deep reverence for their motherland, for India is the most ancient as well as the wisest teacher of humanity. And every child born here has a great responsibility to know, respect and practice the teaching which is so universal and so meaningful.

The friendship that is cultivated from childhood onwards is more lasting, and so, try to cultivate real friends now. Above all, begin the cultivation of virtues. That is more important and beneficial than mere book learning. That gives real bliss. That is the essence of all knowledge, the culmination of all learning. Treat everyone as your own people. Even if you cannot do them any good, desist from causing them any injury. Burn the lamp of love inside the niche of your heart and then, the nocturnal birds of greed and envy will fly away, unable to bear the light. Love makes you humble. It makes you bend and bow when you see greatness and glory.

CHILDREN ARE NOW GROWING UP IN AN ATMOSPHERE

Children are the crops growing in the fields, to yield the harvest on which the nation has to sustain itself. They are the pillars on which the foundation of the nation's future is built. They are the roots of the national tree, which has to give the fruits of work, worship and wisdom to the next generation.

The Sathya Sai Bala Vikas has been evolved in order to feed these roots, strengthen these foundation pillars and fertilize the growing crops. Children are now growing up in an atmosphere polluted by corruption, anxiety and hollow pomp, because people are enamored of the shallow material culture, mainly imported from the West. Parents and teachers and even the leaders of the nation are devoid of admiration and adoration, understanding and practice of the basic principles of Indian Culture. Children are denied the precious heritage which is their due.

Children must grow in the awareness of the brotherhood of man and the Fatherhood of God. If no provision is made for this atmosphere and this teaching, we are denying them their due. Faith in man involves faith in God. Faith in God creates faith in man. Without faith, man is a creature bereft of roots. He dries and withers quickly. Faith in the God within him, who makes him say, I, I, I, when referring to what he was made to say and act and do by the prompting from within, is needed. Faith is the sustenance on which love and courage, contentment and joy grow. Children can be easily made aware of this inner I, which has the body as its apparel. They will grow in mutual love and cooperation with all men of all lands, when they know that color and caste are but apparel which do not affect the real reality.

✣ ✣ ✣ ✣ ✣ ✣ ✣ ✣

BABA SAYS

Pour out all your Love on the children around you and instruct them gladly and sincerely. This attitude alone can justify association with Sathya Sai Bala Vikas.

It is imperative that you should discover the right path and pursue it steadily with faith. Take, for example, the petromax lamp. It requires pumping now and then. We have got to use a pin to clear obstructions, and it must have some quantity of kerosene too. The kerosene is the faith, the pin is the Love which urges you to do your duty, and the will that sustains you in your task. Besides these, the lamp needs wicks. The Name of the God which is your constant inspiration, is the wick. Endeavor, in the light of the Inner Unity of all, to remove the primeval ignorance from yourselves and from your pupils.

CHILDREN'S MINDS ARE ALWAYS OPEN

Children have unselfish Love. They are innocent onlookers. They observe the action of the elders and they learn their lessons from the home much earlier than from school. So, parents have to be careful in their behavior with the children and between themselves.

Children are like fresh cloth. It can be given any color you like. Just a dip in that color, that is enough.

Adults are like old clothes that will not imbibe color so easily and well. Hearts that are raw and soft will learn habits and disciplines quicker. For the learning of good habits and manners, age is no bar; training will make even children learn them.

Adults develop a sense of shame and of pride which is mostly artificial, false and skin deep. And so, they invent excuses to justify their actions and also manufacture justifications for their errors. Children have no such inhibitions. They believe everybody and everybody can believe them. Their hearts are like gramophone records. They get impressed by whatever tune you sing to them. They play back the correct tune, without any distortion, provided the needle is sharp. The needle is Love and it must be pointed and direct. Then only can the music be drawn out. In the case of elders, the needles would have been blunted. Children have the gift of single-mindedness. They are fearless. It is the elders who plant their fears in them. They are truthful, but the elders teach them the art of lying. They set children to spy and report and thus they become interested in the faults and errors of others.

The human heart when young is very soft. It responds to grief and pain in fellow-men. It is the example of elders, the lessons they receive from parents and the company they get into, the training they get in school and society that harden these hearts into stone.

When the elders speak, it is difficult to discover whether it is truth or scandal or untruth. But children are plain-spoken. They have not discovered that success, in the worldly sense, is dependent on cleverness in the short run; though in the long run, it is honesty and plain speaking that bring maximum profit. That is why it is said that you must either become as simple and straight forward as a child or as wise and discriminating as a deeply learned scholar, to win the Grace of God.

Poison and nectar cannot merge. The Real can merge only with the Real. Nature is the Universal Absolute illusion; the Universal Absolute is Nature-illusion! Cloth is yarn illusion and yarn is cloth illusion. One is meaningless without the other. The childhood stage is the pure stage and if you only manage to live on with that innocence as Suka did, you can achieve merger quite naturally. The Sun's rays wait outside your closed door, silently and patiently. Open it to the width of a chink—and it gladly rushes in through that clink. Open it wider, it bathes you in light and warmth. Children's mind are always open. They have no closed doors which bring in the darkness. That is why their smile is sunlight in a grief stricken home.

CHRIST SAID OFTEN THAT BLISS IS PLAYING AROUND THE TENDER CHEEKS OF CHILDREN

Why does man wail when he arrives into the world, whimper throughout his life and groan out, into the beyond, lamenting that his sojourn here was a waste of years? Man does so, because he is unaware of his glory, of his high destiny! He is the Divine poured into the human mold, just as is everything else, alive or inert. But it is the privilege of man alone, to be able to become aware of this precious truth! This is the Message of the Upanishads to Man. This Message is echoed by the scriptures, and in the declarations of countless saints. Yet, man turns a deaf ear to it, perhaps due to his own misfortune created by his own misdeeds in past lives. He can derive bliss through the contemplation of his Divinity, or the Divine as represented by all that he sees, hears, tastes, touches or smells outside himself.

The Absolute is immanent in all. What an inexhaustible source of bliss lies inside or outside you! Only you have to develop the mind that will respond to the call, that will recognize the Truth. The baby in the cradle is the very picture of bliss. When it cries out of grief, we run towards it, for it is against its nature to be sad. Man too is essentially bliss. Misery is alien to his makeup. Divine bliss is the coveted destination for man. We ask ourselves where this bliss is, how does one reach this place of bliss. And what should we do to reach this bliss. The answer has been given by the disciples of Sankara. They said that this bliss is to be found in children who are in ecstasy and who do not have knowledge of their surroundings. As we grow older, we get more and more involved in sensuous desires. We are not thinking even for a little while about the bliss that we experienced in our childhood.

Christ said often that bliss is playing around the tender cheeks of children, in whom there are no desires. Children often exhibit this bliss in a remarkable manner. The bliss and happiness which children show have no parallel in anything else in the world. For example, if a mother is carrying a child and walking on the road, the child sometimes looks back and laughs. Children have got this extraordinary quality in them that they can make elders also laugh. The reason for this is that they are under no illusion about the importance of their bodies. Elders are so much immersed in thinking of their body and things that involve the body that even if they want to laugh, they cannot do so. They only put up a pretense of laughter. It is in this context that the *Bhagavad Gita* says that one who laughs is the Lord Himself and one who cries is man. We laugh only when we are happy. When we are happy, we not only laugh but also try to sing some songs. Those who have a sweet voice will sing in public. Those who do not have a sweet voice will, at least, sing in the bathroom. Krishna had a sweet voice and perfect knowledge of sweet melody and even tempo and so he was singing the Gita even in the battlefield.

Man's life has a beginning and an end, the beginning and the end are both governed by the law of cause and effect. The nest of a bird, built with arduous circumspection on the branch, is swayed by the gale and felled by the storm. The lovely petals of the rose, dancing in the breeze and spreading fragrance around, are blown to the ground by a sudden gust of wind! Man too is floored at the height of his triumph by the stroke of some unseen hand. Man is aghast at the consequence that he experiences. He is unaware of the cause, for he has no inclination to seek it. The cause of birth is the same as the cause for death: fascination for sense-objects and the trail of activity that it involves. Children are happy since they have not yet become involved in such activity. They scatter joy and enthusiasm, innocence and confidence. How is it that they are so fresh and gay? Their minds are free from the infection of sensuous pleasure seeking. They are reveling in the untainted joy of their innate nature. That is the reason why Christ fondled a child, and advised all the grownups to become children so that they may be saved. How sweet is the smile of the baby in the cradle or of the child playing in the garden? That is the genuine nature of man, which he tarnishes foolishly, year by year, as he grows.

In children, the mind is in its native purity; for, they have no sense of "mine." Jesus took the child up and fondling it, carried it on his shoulder. Children are innocent angels. But when they grow up, they start developing desires leading to greed, pride, hate, malice and envy. Thus, peace is lost and fear and anxiety take its place. To regain the peace and joy of childhood, man struggles in devious ways, ways, that lead him deeper and deeper into the morass.

A child in all love. Its smile is most innocent. It has not learnt to work for gains. It has no attachment to the goods of the world. The love-full heart of the child hardens with age because greed breeds hatred and envy.

DISCIPLINE

DISCIPLINE IS THE MARK OF INTELLIGENT LIVING.

DISCIPLINE IS MISSING. HONESTY IS AT A DISCOUNT.

A DISCIPLINED PERSON MUST EXAMINE EVERY ACT TO FIND OUT WHETHER IT WILL CAUSE PAIN TO OTHERS.

BABA SAYS

The friends that the child makes at school and around the home have a beneficial or deleterious effect on his growth. Comics, horror stories, terrorism, gunmen pictures, and cinema posters that degrade man into flesh and skin—these drag the prospective hero into a zero. The child learns to worship money and things which money can buy; he admires cruelty and cunning, rather than sympathy and love. So, the home, the school and the society—all three have to arouse themselves and take up this challenge to the future of this great land.

DISCIPLINE MUST BE TAUGHT

Discipline is the mark of intelligent living. Parents should not allow children to fall away from their control, and wander about without compass or anchor. Many parents feed and fondle their children, and then, in the name of freedom, leave them to find their own friends and pleasures. They take them to films regardless of the impression they create on their tender minds. They entertain the friends of their children, but do not inquire about their antecedents or habits. They even encourage their children to smoke and drink, not knowing they will one day have to rue their action. They thus declare, by their actions, that they are the enemies of their own progeny!

I like children. I take great care of them. I pay them great attention. I give, and advise parents to give them, proper advice at the proper time. I insist on discipline, on reverent obedience to parents, on regulated food and play, on rigorous allocation of time for study, bhajan, meditation, etc. I also recommend some items of service, such as nursing the sick. I condemn frivolous talk, luxurious living, deleterious habits, addiction to films, horror-comics, pen friends, exotic dress, outlandish coiffures designed to draw attention to oneself, etc. By these means, boys and girls are slowly drawn into unrighteous and immoral ways.

Institutions where education is imparted today have no atmosphere of moral or spiritual value. Discipline is missing. Honesty is at a discount. Politeness and good manners are estimated as outmoded forms of behavior. Grab and not give is the rule. Intolerance is held in high esteem.

Discipline trains you to put up with disappointments. You will know that the path of life has both ups and downs, that every rose has its thorn. Now, people want roses without thorns, life has to be one saga of sensual pleasure, a picnic all the time.

When this does not happen, you turn wild and start blaming others.

A disciplined person must examine every act to find out whether it will cause pain to others. If it does, withdraw from it. It is the best test for distinguishing right from wrong. Discipline must be taught so they may develop a broad outlook.

Discipline is important in order to progress in learning and even more so in dealing with others. An undisciplined person is a danger to society, any moment he may run amuck. Man must recognize what limits, regulations and do's and don'ts are laid down, in order to ensure social security and individual advancement.

The Andhra Association can well take up this work—having good company on Saturdays and Sundays and Thursdays where Spiritual discipline for this inner cleanliness can be discovered and practiced. Elders must consider how best they can be exemplars in this field for the young men and women under their care, those who look up to them for guidance, those to whom they are heroes. They must engage themselves in some disciplines like prayer beads and meditation. They must evince enthusiasm and satisfaction in those disciplines. They must be courageous in calamity and take both good and bad as gifts from God. Then only can the children in their care learn to live happily and in peace.

Discipline them with good norms of behavior. They must also learn to follow and to practice good manners at home and outside.

Remember

When Children are equipped with discipline to ensure balance, equanimity, harmony and peace, they cannot be drawn into wild adventures and barren activities.

THERE ARE NO BAD CHILDREN AT ALL

Boarding schools and hostels, where the teachers and wardens are genuinely interested in thus uplifting the coming generation, may succeed more than many homes and most schools. But even they should not try to shape the children into a predetermined mold. Ancient wisdom has no set pattern. It admits of infinite variety, based on past achievement and present accomplishment. It has been suggested that the bad children—there are no bad children at all, there are only ill-brought-up children—should be isolated and given special attention, so that they may be cured of evil tendencies. But I do not like isolating them and directing the attention of everyone to them as specially marked-out boys. It is not good for them, nor is it good for the others. You may pay some special attention to them, unnoticed by the rest of the boys, because they happen to come from families that have no roots in spiritual practice. That is all that is advisable. Of course, a good teacher knows how to manage such students if he or she has faith and intelligence.

There should not be, in My opinion, separate "Moral Instruction" lessons in the curriculum. Every subject has to be learnt, with moral instruction, as the thread running through from lesson to lesson. By example and precept, in the classroom and the playground, the excellence of intelligent cooperation, of sacrifice for the team, of sympathy for the less gifted, of help to the maimed, the weak, the ill and the poor, of love and self-reliance, of silence and prayer, has to be emphasized. The indirect method of instilling these morals is better than direct teaching, through textbooks and tests. Tell stories from the Upanishads and the Bible, from the *Ramayana*, and the lives of Saints from all nations and all the ages, to illustrate a point while doing any lesson, in any subject. It is possible to teach even science and mathematics in either a moral or an immoral way. Prefer the moral way.

One advantage which will accrue when you take this moral uplift program in right earnest is that, through the subtle influence of the children, you are cleansing the atmosphere of the homes also. When the boy sits in silence and meditates on the Maker of all this wonder and glory, the parents too will react in the same way and the atmosphere of the home will be filled with humility and love.

THEY ARE THE GREATEST FOES OF THEIR PROGRESS

The parents must improve themselves, for the sake of their children. Example is more profitable than precept. When the parents have no reverence for God, when the child has to breathe the atmosphere of scandal, faction and greed at home, how can it grow into a happy, healthy, balanced individual? The films that children are taken to see are full of violence and falsehood, mean tricks and conspiracies, which tarnish the springs of sympathy and love. There are parents who are proud when their children join them in card games or even drinking and gambling. There are parents who get angry when their children read religious books, attend temple rites and sit quietly for a few minutes meditating on the awe and wonder that Creation evokes in them. If the parent is a drunkard, a gambler, and a cheat, no amount of textbook ethics can cure the son.

How can such parents claim to be the well-wishers of their progeny? They are the greatest foes of their progress They do not equip their children with the armor which will render them safe in the turmoil of life. They try to make their children unworthy of the name, Indian; for they grow up without learning about Rama or Krishna or the Gita or the *Bhagavatha*! They toil to leave their children a pile of riches; but they do not teach them the proper sense of values, by which they can know how little the riches are worth, or how best to utilize the riches for their genuine advancement. They must be taught to live like lotuses in the lake of Change, being in water but unaffected by it. Lotuses cannot live when out of water; but yet, they will not allow water to enter! Be in Change, but see that Change is not in you. That is the secret of successful living, which they do not teach the young.

I will not allow them to be blamed. The fault lies wholly on the shoulders of the elders who shape the norms which they imbibe.

The hearts of children are unsullied by sensual desires. Teachers and parents, comrades, and elders, spoil them by their conduct and example. They tarnish their immaculate nature. If only they are allowed to grow in the proper spiritual atmosphere, if they are allowed to approach God, then they become good, just, humble and pure. That does not mean they will be weak. They will be strong with all the strength of Truth. Then, they will be invaluable assets to the nation. But now, when schools are denied the spiritual atmosphere, they grow up into handicaps on the road to progress, problems to themselves as well as to the nation. This is the reason why I have entered the field of education, and established colleges for the new era, for both boys and girls, in different states.

✣✣✣✣✣✣✣✣

TENDER SAPLINGS

"Student Inmates,

Though you have to observe a rather strict regimen of duties in this institution, you should find in your stay here a valuable opportunity to mold your lives and shape your character for the better, while there is time. A sapling can be helped to grow straight, but once it becomes a tree it cannot be guided in its growth. In childhood, you were led astray because you did not know which act was right and which wrong. There was no one to guide you along the good path. You fell into bad company because no one warned you, or rescued you when you had done so. No one pointed out to you the way to God and goodness. If they had, you would have quickly absorbed the advice, for the minds of children are capable of imbibing the good as well as the bad. No one around you had faith in your innate Divinity, or the compassion to save you from evil and guide you into good ways.

Well, forget the past. It has already elapsed. The present is the most important time for us. Hold on to truth, and follow the right path now. Utter truth, act virtuously, say the Vedas. Do not entertain thoughts of despair or dejection. Be happy that you have this chance of rebuilding yourselves into fine boys and girls with lovable manners and behavior. These people from the Seva Samithi come to you and through devotional songs and prayer raise an atmosphere of love and mercy. They tell you of God, the *Avatar* and saints. Have Ramakrishna and Vivekananda as your ideals. Follow their examples. In this institution they give you a training that will liberate you, unlike the training which you had when you were children and which put you in bondage. Absorb the lessons you are taught here to the fullest possible extent and put into practice the guidance given to you.

Do not have any ill feeling amongst yourselves. Help others when they need your help and when you can really help them. Do not think that it is enough if you just sing the glory of God when the people from the Seva Samithi come and join you. Sing them in your minds, silently, sincerely, even when you are walking or working, writing or making calculations. The name of God is like a torch that guides your steps in the dark. Suppose you have to walk through a forest in the night, you may wonder how a little torch can help you through such a long journey in the dark. Well, when you walk with the torch in your hand, the light it sheds walks with you. So also in the long journey of life through the night of ignorance, the name of God on your tongue acts like a torch light, bright and clear, to direct your every successive step.

Resolve to be good, lovable children from his moment. Do your duties gladly and well, to the satisfaction of your well-wishers. If you feel sorry for the wrongs you did, that itself will please God and He will pardon you. If you endeavor to turn a new leaf and become better, God will shower Grace on you. Here you are given protection and education and an opportunity to learn how to be useful sons and daughters of your great land. Whenever an idea of hurting others, or taking someone else's belongings, or spreading falsehood about others enters your mind, turn to God for help. Ask Him to give you strength. For all these ideas are born of fear and cowardice, qualities which in turn come from weakness. Repeat the name of God or hum a devotional song and you will find that all your bad thoughts would have fled, leaving you free from evil.

When you leave this institution, you must serve as examples for others by leading active useful lives. This is a workshop where you have come like cars damaged through ignorance and neglect. You must leave the institution in fine running condition, rid of all your faults and attractive in appearance and character. Your kith and kin, your friends, the elders of your village, and all who have the welfare of our country at heart, must be happy and proud to see you acquiring new skills, fine character and eagerness to serve others."

Remand Home, Hyderabad, 10 March 1978

✣✣✣✣✣✣✣✣

BY THE PRESENT GENERATION

This moral code, the product of centuries of selfless pursuit of individual and social contentment, is now thrown to the winds, by the present generation. Sons clamor for a share in the property of the father, but not for a share in his love. They close their ears to their needs and commands. Parents have conferred this physical equipment called body, with which we can attain the Absolute, serve God in all living beings, glorify Him in and through Beauty and Truth, this equipment which is essential for liberating ourselves from the direst of bondage. So gratitude and honor are due to them from children. An iron box is essential to keep safe precious stones. So too, the body is essential to keep safe the precious gifts of virtue, faith, love and discrimination. The parents gave it and so, they have to be respected by speech, action and behavior. How can you expect the Heavenly Father to respond to your prayers if you do not respond to the demands of the earthly Father? The first step in Righteousness is Gratitude. The first duty of the child is reverence to the parents. When the first step is absent, ascent is impossible.

One thing more: Do not do anything which brings tears into the eyes of your parents. Honor them and obey them. Do not condemn them as old-fashioned. "Old is Gold." They speak out of a longer experience of the world and its tricks.

Gratitude to parents is a basic virtue, reverence to the parents is reverence to the past, to the great treasure of wisdom that the past has learned and preserved.

MOTHER COMES FIRST

Love for the mother has to be fostered by everyone. Today this love is prompted more by greed—desire for wealth and gold than by spontaneous affection for the mother. Barely one in a million realizes that he owes his food, blood and life itself to the mother. Whoever she may be, a mother is verily divine. It is said: Regard the mother as God, the father as God, the preceptor as God and the guest as God. The mother stands foremost among these four. She is indeed the first teacher for everyone. It is only the mother who strives most for securing the well-being of the child by showering on it boundless affection and love and showing it the father. Children today do not care to heed their mother's commands but they hanker after the mother's wealth. What is the use of having children of this kind? They are a curse on the womb that bore them.

"Of what use is a son who does not lift both his hands in prayer to the Lord, who does not proclaim the Lord's name with his mouth till it aches, and who does not cherish the Lord in his heart? He is a disgrace to the woman that bore him."

GRATITUDE IS PRIMARY

Every man is prone to commit mistakes either wittingly or unwittingly. But one mistake he should not commit, in any circumstance, is to forget what he owes to his mother. Love of the mother can redeem a man's life, whatever his other lapses may be. The greatest gift of the parents is the body with all its power. Although the Lord rules over all lives, it is the parents who have endowed the body to the child. Clay and water are gifts of Nature. But it is the potter who makes pots out of them. Hence gratitude to the parents is a primary obligation. Students these days ask: why should we be grateful to our parents? They should remember that if they cause distress to these parents now by their behavior, they should not be surprised if in later years their own children cause them similar distresses. This is the law of action and reaction that is always at work. Do not get conceited because of your youth, your wealth or strength. All these are transient. Adi Sankaracharya warned in strident language: Do not get proud because of companions, wealth or youth. Time will take away all these in a moment. Placing their trust in these transitory possessions, men are forgetting the eternal verities and the source of real bliss. Whatever things you may possess, whatever amenities you may enjoy, only faith in God will confer real peace of mind. An air conditioner may cool your body. But only the grace of God can cool the heated brain and the troubled heart. That grace will come to those who are grateful to their parents and render loving service to them. Starting with the mother, gratitude should extend to the father and the preceptor. If you show gratitude to these three, you will realise the presence of the Triune Lord in whom and you will reap the fruit of worshipping the Trinity (Brahma, Vishnu and Shiva.)

Everyone should treasure in his heart love for the mother, who has borne him, reared him with love and fostered him with care. The person who forfeits the mother's love will not earn anyone's love.

THE INNOCENCE OF A CHILD

Baba Says:

Children are innocent Angels. It is such innocence and purity that we have to possess in our hearts.

Children must listen to the words of their mothers. Mothers should avoid putting ideas in the children. When there are such exemplary mothers and children, the world will be full of joy and festivities.

Ramakrishna Paramahamsa said: If you want to pray to God, be like an innocent child.

Jesus also said the same thing when He told His disciple: "Suffer little children to come unto Me, for of such is the Kingdom of Heaven."

Christ fondled a child, and advised all the grownups to become children so that they can be saved.

He also used to say: "Even if I am like a child for even a brief moment in a day how pure can I become."

Jesus Christ said often that the bliss is playing around the tender cheeks of the children, in whom there are no desires.

The disciple of Sankara said:

Bliss is to be found in children who are in ecstasy and who do not have knowledge of their surroundings.

THE INNER BEAUTY OF CHILDREN

Children have the sense of wonder, fresh and free.

The Bliss that radiates from the faces of the children is evidence of their innate simplicity and sweetness.

They are revelling in the untainted joy of their innate nature.

A child is all love; its smile is most innocent.

That is why their smiles are sunlight in a grief-stricken home.

Children have unselfish love.

Children are plain spoken.

They are fearless. They are truthful.

They believe everybody and everybody can believe them.

Children's mind are always open. They have no closed doors which bring in the darkness.

In the tender hearts of the children there is much potentiality of devotion and attachment to higher ideals and objectives This can be developed and cultivated by you.

Children are the crops growing in the fields to yield the harvest on which the nation has to sustain itself.

They are the pillars on which the foundation of the nation's future is built.

Children are now growing up in an atmosphere polluted by corruption, anxiety and hollow pomp.

Children hearts are pure, steady and inclusive. Elders should so behave that they do not tarnish their hearts or make them narrow and vengeful. They must encourage them and soften them through intensive social service.

Children are denied the precious heritage which is their due.

The children take the nation along with them to perdition or progress.

Children do not say one thing and do the opposite. They are too forward and innocent.

Children are wayward and vile, today since they have no other example to follow.

The child is denied the most health-giving vitamin, Love. The home where the fragrance of this Love has to be inhaled has now lost its sacred atmosphere.

Christ said, let children come unto me. They have the sense of wonder, fresh and free.

Children are innocent angels. But when they grow up, they start developing desires leading to greed, pride, hate, malice and envy.

Thus, peace is lost and fear and anxiety take its place.

The human heart when young is very soft. It responds to grief and pain in fellow-men.

Keep those hearts soft. Learn to share with others their grief and their joy.

Parents take them to films regardless of the impression they create on their tender minds.

Children must also learn, follow and practice good manners at home and outside and good norms of behavior.

The mother should teach them that whatever they eat, they should eat it after offering it to God. In the absence of such practice, the conduct of the children is taking a very distorted path.

Lead the children along the joyous path of Truth.

Children must grow up in the atmosphere of reverence, devotion, mutual service and cooperation.

The hearts of children are unsullied by sensual desires.

The child does not crave to posses and to deny others.

The child may have a dirt covered body, but its mind is free of dirt. Elders are scrupulous about physical cleanliness, but their minds are cesspools of desire, of hate, envy and clogging slush.

Bliss is to be found in children who are in ecstasy and who do not have knowledge of their surroundings.

Christ said often that bliss is playing around the tender cheeks of children, in whom there is no desire.

Children often exhibit this bliss in a remarkable manner.

The bliss and happiness which children show have no parallel in anything else in the world.

Children have got this extraordinary quality in them that they can make elders also laugh.

The reason for this is that they are under no illusion about the importance of their bodies.

The children's minds are free from the infection of sensuous-pleasure-seeking.

That is the reason why Christ fondled a child, and advised all the grownups to become children so that they can be saved.

Children are revelling in the untainted joy of their innate nature.

Children's minds are in their native purity; for they have no sense of mine.

A child is all love; his smile is most innocent. He has not learned to work for gain.

The child has no attachment to the goods of the world.

Children have unselfish Love. They are innocent onlookers they observe the action of the elders and they learn their lesson from the home much earlier than from school.

The elders do not distinguish between a cinema hall, a market or an exhibition but talk and chatter everywhere, even in a temple, or a holy gathering.

Children learn from them and they too, when they grow up, lose all reverence for elders and holy places.

Children have the gift of single-mindedness.

They are fearless. It is the elders who plant their fears in them.

They are truthful, but the elders teach them the art of lying.

They set children to spy and report and thus they become interested in the faults and error of others.

When the elders speak, it is difficult to discover whether it is truth or scandal or untruth.

But children are plain-spoken. That is why it is said that you must either become as simple and straight-forward as a child or as wise and discriminating as a deeply learned scholar, to win the Grace of God.

The character of the children must be made strong and pure. Give them all the confidence and courage they need to become good, honest, self-reliant children.

Children are straight forward and innocent. Imbibe this nature now from them; for, elders have strayed far from that ideal.

Children are like fresh cloth. It can be given any color you like. Just dip in that color, that is enough.

Adults are like old clothes that will not imbibe color so easily and well.

Children's minds are innocent, tender and pure.

Children are lamps which can illumine the path of the nation.

Children have to be led into good ways of living life, into simplicity, humility and discipline.

Children have to revere their parents. That is their duty.

Love can bind children together, for they have not yet learned to hate.

Love can similarly, unite all mankind; provided man is cured of greed, envy, desire, and attachment.

Children believe your words when you say that the policeman will catch them or the ghost will beat them.

They are full of fear, humility, and faith.

Children are like realized souls without attachment.

Let the children contemplate the beauties and the magnificence of God's Handiwork and be filled with the mystery and awe.

Let the children learn the recitation of the Name and prayer and the practice of silence.

BABA SAYS

Children are like realized Souls without attachment. Above all, realise that children are precious treasures.

DON'T

Do not presume that the child is some inferior personality or that he is incapable of attaining the heights.

Do not think that they do not know anything; that you can divert them any way you wish. This is a mistake.

Do not burden the tender brains with all sorts of lumber, bits of information that can never be put to use, facts that warp the strands of truth.

Do not sow hatred or contempt of any class, faith or cult in the virgin minds of the little ones.

Do not tarnish the spotlessly clean minds of the children by infecting them with a sense of distinction between one child and another.

Do not set bad examples for the children to follow. Children are wayward and vile, today, since they have no other examples to follow. Teachers, parents, comrades and elders spoil them.

Do not ridicule your children when they show an inclination to visit a temple or a holy hermit.

Don't allow the virus of vice to infect their brains.

Don't read horror comic books on crime and sex, and novels of vice and wickedness.

Do not fall into the traps of anger, jealousy and pride.

Do not crave for the property of others or for things that can be got by trickery or dishonorable means. Earn by the sweat of your brow. Then you can be proud and happy.

Do not set bad examples for these children to follow. If you are truthful, just be calm under provocation and full of love in all your dealings with others. These children too will grow up in Truth and Righteousness, Peace and Love.

Remember

There are no bad children at all. There are only ill brought up children.

BALA VIKAS

The Bala Vikas is the primary basis of the great movement to restore Righteousness in the World.

The ideal of the Bala Vikas is raising a generation of boys and girls who have clean and clear consciousness.

The first thing to be taught to the children is to get into their hearts the need and the method by which they can respect their mother and father at home, conduct themselves and give a shape to the home in which they live. This is what has to be put into their hearts.

In the Bala Vikas we should concentrate on moral and spiritual education only.

The Bala Vikas children whom you are guiding and inspiring will be the leaders of tomorrow in this land.

Think also of the activities that should be promoted through Bala Vikas which can ensure happiness and harmony for the children in later life.

The Bala Vikas classes can serve children of all faiths. You must be careful not to encourage or entertain the slightest trace of difference on the basis of religion, caste, creed or color in the Bala Vikas classes.

The home in which the Bala Vikas children grow, as indeed all homes, have to be clean and with vibrations free from hatred, envy, greed, spite and hypocrisy.

We should not try to give the normal worldly training which is already given normally in the schools.

We should not duplicate and give them the usual worldly training, but confine ourselves to the ethical, moral and spiritual aspect of a child's growth.

In the Bala Vikas classes you must try to have children from various faiths so that friendships between them can grow into understanding, and understanding into LOVE.

Instruct the children of the Bala Vikas to revere their parents. That is their duty.

As teacher of the Bala Vikas classes you do not look to monetary or material benefits; so you have ample opportunity to make the child's heart and intellect blossom, through the rays of Love.

All the teachers should regard the children in the Bala Vikas as their own children. They should look after them in the manner in which a mother will look after her own children.

Bala Vikas children must have fear, humility and faith: Fear of doing wrong, of falling into falsehood, humility before elders, teachers, parents, faith in God, in your own strength, in your own victory.

TEACHERS

The profession of a teacher is the most responsible one in every country.

The teachers are the lamps from which these tender hearts must receive light and love.

Teachers are reservoirs from which through the process of education, students draw the water of life.

BABA SAYS

Most teachers have been rendered materialistic, worldly and egoistic. They do not know that real education consists in helping the child to manifest the Divinity latent in him. Remember that the children, who come to you, are all heirs to the richest cultural heritage that the world can give.

The teacher who instructs pupils with the eye fixed on his salary, and the pupil who learns with the eye on a job are both missing their vocation.

The teacher has to help the pupil unfold and manifest the skills and qualities inherent in him and encourage him to rise to the fullest height he is capable.

The Divine is the core in both teacher and pupil.

BABA SAYS

The difference between the ancient ideals of education and the modern practices is appalling. Today the educational process is denied to the aspirant if he fails to pay his fees. The teacher too feels that he has no duty to teach if in a certain month he is not paid his salary. Students pay for being taught. Teachers are paid for the teaching they do. Money decides what is taught and how it is learnt.

"Pay and receive, be paid and give."

That is the bond between the teacher and the taught. Love, reverence, affection—these have no place in the transaction. How then can education be fruitful? When material gain is the goal, the joy is based on matter and does not thrill the mind. It cannot be pure, steady and sincere.

TEACHERS

UNDER THE GURU

As days pass by, the process of reshaping and reforming affects each field. Naturally, it is being applied to the educational system also. In former times, children were initiated in the spiritual path at the proper age and their studies began thereafter, under the Guru or Preceptor.

In the past, teachers saw to it that the pupils were equipped with devotion to God in addition to the curricular training. So, the students were well versed in spiritual discipline and knowledge. Every act of theirs was motivated by the yearning for salvation and spiritual joy.

Boys and girls were instructed by gurus who had full knowledge of the country—its history, and traditions—and the principles of religion and culture. Now, since the teachers are themselves woefully ignorant of what culture means, what spirituality consists of, and what the significance of religion is, the pupils are deprived of the wisdom that alone can confer peace and joy to their hearts.

The propaganda for atheism, the declaration that the Vedas have no historical validity, and the teaching through history that Hinduism is destroyed—these are the activities of the teachers who suffer from the mania for Western culture and civilization.

Can we call such a system of instruction, education? Can we call those who instruct these things, gurus? Education is the communication of the knowledge of the Divine power, and the inner Reality of the Self. This alone justifies the claim to be educated.

Since they have no spiritual awareness, students are taking part in disorders and disturbances. They become easy targets to mob violence, unworthy of the educated. They descend to levels lower than the blind reach in their ignorance and draw down upon themselves the ridicule of the observers. They disfigure the educational institutions and bring disgrace upon them.

We have heard the Guru being praised as equal to God. The Guru sows the seeds of virtue, of wisdom, and of faith in the heart of the pupil. The Guru cannot sit back and silently watch the fate of the pupil, after the first few lessons. He has to guide the pupil at every step, foster and encourage good habits, sound reasoning and valid emotions.

The Guru has also the duty cast on him, to watch every step of the pupil, and warn him off, when he takes a false step, or develops a bad habit, or entertains a deleterious doubt. Like the farmer who has to be vigilant against the growth of weeds or the upsurge of pests, the Guru too must be ever alert to destroy the pests of vice and the weeds of sloth and unsteadiness. The word "teacher" cannot denote these high roles. It can mean only those who transmit information and train in skills. I direct that Bala Vikas teachers should hereafter be known by the vastly more appropriate name, "Guru," so that you may be conscious always of the spiritual role which you have taken on and its responsibilities, and value. You are the lamps from which these tender hearts must receive Light and Love. By your adherence to Truth, Righteousness, Peace and Love, you have to inspire these qualities in the children who come to you and the homes from where they come.

Be conscious of the sacred significance of the name *guru,* by which you are known. "Gu" means "darkness" "ru" means "removal." So the guru has to illumine the intelligence of the child and remove the ignorance that is obstructing its full development. Diving deeper, we find that *guru* has another meaning also. "Gu" means "not limited by attributes" and "ru" means "not affected by appearances." That is to say, the guru must be free from preferences and prejudices and must treat all the pupils with equal Love. Love can, similarly unite all mankind; provided man is cured of greed, envy, desire, and attachment. The guru should point to his pupils the common factor of good advice about human conduct contained in the scriptures of all religions. The Guru must teach him a standard of values, with which to deal with the family, the village, the community, the country and mankind.

✣✣✣✣✣✣✣✣

AS THE TEACHER, SO THE PUPIL

Gurus have to be examples which can inspire the pupils. They must practice what they preach. As the teacher, so the pupil. When the tap is turned water flows only if the overhead tank is full. The quality of tap water is the same as that of the water in the tank. When the heart of the *guru* is full of goodness, selflessness and Love, the pupils will express these virtues in every act of theirs.

There are, it is said, more than 5000 *Bala Vikas gurus* in the land. If each one corrects and improves a hundred children, the nation would indeed be transformed. You must examine what exactly has been attained during the four years that have elapsed since Bala Vikas came into being. This analytical study has to be made constantly. When the *guru* cultivates a pure nature, students too will grow into embodiments of that nature.

The *guru* should be alert that the weeds of hatred, envy and similar vices do not take root in her own heart. These weeds are mainly rampant in the political fields. Teachers should not form rival groups—some proud of their achievements, some envious of the praise others earn—which engage themselves in recrimination. See others as your own brothers and sisters, for all are one when viewed as Self.

There are many who shiver at the prospect, when they contemplate the future of this great country. You should never entertain such doubts and fears, for you are builders of that future and you know that it will be glorious. The Bala Vikas children whom you are guiding and inspiring will be the leaders of tomorrow in this land. The virtues you implant in them, the counsel you are providing them, the examples you place before them will remain carved in their memories and transform their outlook and behavior in the days to come. Ask anyone assembled here whether he can bring back to memory the book that he read this morning. Ninety-five per cent of this vast gathering will fail in this test. But ask them to repeat from memory some one hymn or stotra or other verse that their grandfather or grandmother taught them when they were little children sitting on their knees; and I am sure ninety-five per cent of them will be able to recite the sloka or stotra. The things learnt during those early years stick in the memory and act subtly and silently on the growing mind to modify and purify the conduct of later years.

Teaching is a process in which the teacher and the taught co-operate and it must be a pleasant experience for both, a useful and heartening endeavor. Kshana means second and I want that you must learn a good lesson every second of your school life. For example, when the teacher enters the classroom, children salute him. That is a lesson in humility, in respecting age and scholarship, in gratitude for services rendered. The should decide to deserve the salutations of the children entrusted to his care by sincere work and selfless service. The student must not respect the teacher through fear, but must be moved more by love. The teacher should avoid all methods that frighten, or terrorise.

Education

Education is a slow process like the unfoldment of a flower, the fragrance becoming deeper and more perceptible with the silent blossoming, petal by petal, of the entire flower.

The unfolding will be helped if the teacher is a fine example of Renunciation, Humility and Discrimination rather than a person engaged in the task of mere teaching and coaching for examinations. Example, not precept, is the best teaching aid.

THE HOLIEST TASK

The ideals of the Bala Vikas movement are the highest. The task of fulfilling them is the holiest of tasks. Knowing this but yet not doing one's best, is indeed treason to oneself. Mere talk cannot go far. Man in concerned with the moon that is hundreds of thousands of miles away, but he is not concerned with his nearest neighbour. Do not instruct or instil in children, magnificent ideas and colossal thoughts. Teach them small, practical ideas and simple items of behavior through your own example and loving exposition.

Only the teacher of teachers can direct the Bala Vikas guru. That is to say, he who has mastered the process and problems and the significance and secrets of education, can so direct.

Of course our Bala Vikas gurus should not indulge in jealousy or fault-finding. They can undertake the task of teaching only after they rid themselves of evil traits. If gurus talk ill of other gurus and promote misunderstanding and factionalism, the children can never improve. So resolve now to adhere to the right path.

If two gurus quarrel or become unfriendly, both will be removed. No inquiry is necessary. We condemn both for having been involved. One poisonous insect can destroy an entire crop.

Since we have not been very strict all these years, we find the number of Bala Vikas pupils is very low, even with such a large number of gurus. Each guru must serve at least a hundred pupils in one year, only then can we have at least a hundred thousand or more getting the benefit. There are nine crores [ten milion] and twenty-six thousand children, boys and girls in our country, aged below ten. Those below sixteen are twenty-two crores six hundred thousand in number. At the rate at which we are training the children, when can we teach the crores? The present tortoise speed will not help.

I would advice you to pay special attention to the methods by which you can contribute, through the Bala Vikas, to the blossoming of the talents latent in the children, the expansion of the prosperity of the nation and the security and welfare of society. Think also of the activities that should be promoted through the Bala Vikas which can ensure happiness and harmony for the children in later life. Children are lamps which can illumine the path of the nation.

THE PROFESSION OF A TEACHER IS THE MOST RESPONSIBLE ONE IN EVERY COUNTRY

We now believe that the acquisition of knowledge is for the acquisition of wealth. But this is not right. Education is really related to the very consummation of life. It has to do with the goal of life more than the means of living. It is only through education and more education that we can instil into the mind of man the sacred ideals of human life.

By education a young man gains a degree which is only another name for the bowl to be used for begging for jobs! Indian education should ideally emphasise self-reliance and independent living. It should confer on the student the courage to stand up against injustice, indiscipline, immorality and falsehood. It should grant steady faith in the Self as the reality of man.

The profession of a teacher is the most responsible one in every country. If the teacher strays from the path of truth, the entire society will suffer. So you must make every effort to live life uprightly. You have in your charge, looking up to you for guidance, children so innocent that they have no knowledge yet of the world and its ways. It is only when the teacher himself is wedded to discipline and observes good habits that his pupils will be able to shape themselves into ideal individuals and citizens. When the teacher falls a victim to bad habits, undesirable manners, bad company and evil behavior, the children too will naturally be drawn into evil ways. If the teacher sets an evil example before his pupils, it may happen that his students turn against him and use against him the evil that they learnt from him. Thus the teacher has to bear the responsibility of promoting the welfare of the world or bringing the world down to disaster. Of course, even today there are some teachers who follow the ancient ideals. Indian culture is even today fresh and green only because there are in the country some teachers filled with holy feelings and sacred ideals.

Really speaking, teachers who got the chance to attend this camp are fortunate. You have been assigned the duty of moulding the children of your schools into ideal pupils. Every village school is to be transformed into a hermitage and every teacher into a Sage who will lead the children along material, moral, ethical and spiritual paths, until they become ideal citizens of India. You too belong to the line of the ancient Sages because you have been chosen for this task. What has happened today, is the disappearance of the Sage from the hermitage, so that it has become the miserable school!

You should not give room for any doubt and discussion on religious matters. You must recognise the truth that can reconcile and bring together all religions without distinction. Teach the children this truth and instil love and harmony in the tender minds of boys and girls. They are now lovely creepers who depend on you and your care for their growth and blossoming.

The holy undertaking has been started by the chief minister and the minister for education. They have planted the sapling. You, teachers, are entrusted with the duty of tending it and making it grow into a fine tree which will offer its flowers and fruits of the world. You must help the flower of peace to blossom and the fruit of spiritual equanimity to be shared by all mankind. In fact you are not merely teachers at your own schools, but are teachers of the human race.

Therefore you have to cultivate in your own heart the spirit of sacrifice, the virtues of charity and the awareness of Divinity. Then only do you become entitled to cultivate these in the hearts of the children. But unfortunately these principles of Indian cultural education are absent from schools today. You must try your best to reshape the system and make it really Indian Culture. Of course in the initial stages you will find this task very difficult and exhausting, but be assured that as you proceed you will find your task more and more easy.

HOW TO BRING OUT THE SPLENDOR OF DIVINITY

In the coming days we will take up each subject and the possibilities and implications of teaching it. Out of these discussions will emerge resolutions and programmes which we can all consider later. During these ten days each day will be devoted to the consideration of one aspect of spiritual and cultural education. How to develop the attitude of Love among the children? How to make them recognise the kinship that unites all mankind? How to implant in their minds feelings against caste distinctions, regional differences and religious prejudices? How to bring out the splendor of Divinity that is the core of humanity? These topics have to be given special attention.

In schools we have teachers who teach history or geography or mathematics. The geography teacher opens out a map and points to some country and explains how people live there. The mathematics teacher writes on the blackboard 3+3+3=9. The history teacher relates the story of a ruler. But the drill teacher has to stand before the lined-up pupils and himself demonstrate what they should do when he says one, two, three, four, etc. Every teacher has, like the drill teacher, to *do* what he says. He must demonstrate in his own life the truth and validity of what he advises the pupils to do. For example, he punishes them for smoking *beedies* and cigarettes. But when he is himself addicted to smoking, what authority has he to advise others against it? By this type of hypocrisy the teacher loses all respect in the eyes of his pupils. If, however, you observe the rules you impose and then try to put them in practice, your advise will be certain to be followed. When can you reach this stage? It is possible only when you become at least embodiments of human-ness, and when you recognise what the essential human qualities are.

The thought that arises in the mind, the word that is formed on the tongue and the act performed by the hand—when these three form stages of the same process they indicate human-ness. Nowadays, man *appears* to be man, but his human-ness is absent, partly because he thinks one way, speaks another way and acts a third way. Speak what you think. Do what you speak. **That is the sign of the true Manhood.**

So you must first act according to your own advice bring about consonance between your thought, word and deed, and then guide the children. Otherwise you, as teachers, cannot cut much ice with them.

Through the centuries India has nursed many religions, creeds and sects. But the essence of all Scriptures is the one truth that in every being there exists the Divine. The teaching of this essence is very necessary today. As the minister for education said just now, the foundation of an edifice has to be very strong. Even a small house requires a foundation. For a tree to grow, the roots have to be strong indeed. Without roots the tree will collapse with the first gust of wind. A house without a foundation will fall down in a heap with the very first gust of wind. Similarly, pupils in schools must have for their satisfactory progress in life, a strong foundation. And what is a strong foundation? Moral ethical and spiritual knowledge and experience are the best foundation.

If man wishes to be happy and healthy, the first exercise he must do is to remove from his mind every bad thought, feeling and habit. What is the next step? He must welcome good thoughts, good feelings and good habits. These exercises can be started even from childhood. Removing the bad and substituting it with the good has to be done by you as a teacher for your public. You must be vigilant to prevent the children from being spoiled by the evils of injustice, violence, immorality and falsehood. These are the austerities imposed on you as your duty.

YOU HAVE TO SERVE THEM AS YOUR OWN CHILDREN

This bliss does not come out of books, nor can it be bought for any sum. It can be got only by dedicated work.

Embodiments of Love! I wish very much that you should fill your hearts with Love and lead the children under your care along the path of Indian ideals. For this you have to form study groups in order to collect and codify your suggestions.

Whatever one learns or does not learn, he must, after being born as man, learn about the Self for that alone can give him bliss and immorality.

Resolve today to sacrifice everything you have for the sake of the pure-hearted children who rely on you for guidance. So long as you are caught in the coils of monetary considerations and so long as you think that such benefit alone can make you happy, you will continue to be as you are. But can you gain bliss the very day you decide on dedicated service? Whether you get or do not get the comforts you require, you should pay attention to the task for which you have come and cultivate the means for realizing the Self.

Teachers must be conscious of their responsibility to set examples to the students. When one teacher neglects her duty or lowers her standard of conduct, hundreds of students are affected thereby. The moral strength and virtues of the teachers will be reflected in the students on whom they exercise the impact. You have to serve them as your own children, children who need and deserve your Love. Be like mothers to these children and let this college be ringing with Love given and Love received.

Pour out all your Love on the children around you and instruct them gladly and sincerely. More than all, fill your mind with God and transmit God to the Children.

Baba Says

The children you claim to be yours are born out of lust, but the children who come to you for education are drawn to you by your Love. Believe that more than your physical children, these children have a right to your Love. So decide to make the sacrifice for the sake of the pure-hearted children who rely on you for guidance.

THE TEACHER PLAYS THE MOST IMPORTANT ROLE

Though this area and this town are not new to Me, this is the first time that most of you are seeing Me. When a few more dishes are prepared, it becomes a Festival day. So, when the District Athletic Competitions are held here, it is a Festival for the boys and students as well as for parents and others interested in the welfare of the country. You have all put on a glad face, forgetting the daily drudgery. You have witnessed the competitions and the games and enjoyed the keenness and enthusiasm of the participants. The students sitting before us are the instruments with which the India of tomorrow is to be shaped. Their teachers, who are also here, are indeed lucky, for destiny has allotted them the noble task, the golden chance, to serve the interests of the people in this pleasant manner, spending their time in the company of innocent, fresh children. The father, the mother and teacher are the three primarily responsible for molding the future of the country. Of these, the teacher plays the most important role, for he is specially trained and selected for the job. He voluntarily takes it up and therefore must carry it out to the best of his ability without demur. He is implicitly trusted by the child, the parents and the public alike and the trust must be repaid by honest service. He is honored and respected by the children and the public as the Guru, with all the hallowed associations of that word. He may be poor, uncared for by the men at the top, but the satisfaction he gets by his quiet creative work is enough compensation. The teacher must never curse his pupils whatever the provocation. He must always bless them. If he swears like a boor, he reduces himself to the level of a boor.

He should watch his behavior rigorously, and find out whether there is some habit or trait which, if imitated by the pupil, will be harmful. He must himself follow the advice that he gives. Otherwise, he will be teaching hypocrisy to the little children and encouraging them to acquire the cleverness not to be found out. It is sheer mental weakness and cowardice that allow hypocrisy to develop. If you have the courage to face the consequence, you will never utter falsehood.

A Bad Teacher Ruins The Career Of Hundreds

A bad pupil causes harm only to himself. A bad teacher ruins the career of hundreds. Be steady and stable in your efforts. A guidepost which changes direction with every gust of wind adds only confusion to the confounded traveler. You have also to cultivate love and expand your desire to do seva (service).

The teacher should not try to rule through the easier means of fear, for, that is full of dangerous consequences on the pupils. Try rather the path of Love. Teachers should themselves take to the discipline of Prayer beads and Meditation. This will give them the inner quiet they sorely need. They should create an atmosphere of plain living and high thinking, for pupils unconsciously accept them as heroes and begin imitating them. They must hand over to the rising generation the riches that past generations have amassed, viz., the spiritual disciplines and discoveries. Learn them yourselves and teach them to the pupils under your care. This will enable you to discharge the debt due from you to the rishis of old. I know that when you sow bitter seeds you cannot grow sweet grain. But yet, there are certain things possible even under the limitations of the present curricula and courses of study.

The unmistakable sign of rain is the wetness of the ground. So too, the sign of a person who has had some years of schooling is good manners. He must have humility, that the field of knowledge is so vast and he has been unable even to touch its fringe. He must be aware of his kinship with all mankind and he must show a keenness to do service to others at all times, gladly and without desire for publicity. The educated boy must move with others in a free and friendly way. God is the moving force in everyone. He is behind all good impulses and useful attitudes. You are all separate beads strung together on that one thread, God. So hatred is ugly, unnatural and inhuman. It is against the very core of love that is in everyone. Always respect another's opinion and another's point of view. Don't start a quarrel at the slightest difference of opinion. He may be right and you may be wrong. Ponder over his argument. He might have had the advantage of knowing more about the subject or you may be prejudiced either for or against. Or he may not know as much as you. All difference of opinion is not due to personal hatred, remember.

The guru should not give way to conceit in his heart. As the indispensable teacher of innocent, illiterate and half-blind children, the Guru should not occupy a chair of authority. Egoism is the throne which is proudly appropriated by authority. Be humble before the children and renounce the tone of power. This in the Spiritual discipline for you. Revere the role of a guru as a Blessing from GOD. This attitude alone can ensure the success of the journey for the individual, the society and the world.

The teacher—that is the more correct appellation—should not feel superior. The pupil should not feel inferior. Both are Self in reality. There is no high and no low. All are waves in the ocean of Bliss.

Lead the children along the joyous path of Truth. Let your faces ever shower smiles, springing from the bliss you earn from the faces of the children. Let them sing songs that glorify God. Do not fall into the traps of anger, jealousy, and pride. You can avoid them through steady and sincere attention to the task you have undertaken. May the children you serve become heroes in the revival of the ancient glory of the motherland.

I like children, I insist on discipline, on reverent obedience to parents, discipline is important in order to progress

Baba Says

The school is always a house of God. To treat it as a caravansary or a prison or a house of correction, is sacrilege. Treat it as a holy place, where the Goddess of Learning, the deity presiding over knowledge and the arts, is worshipped. Then, in that atmosphere of veneration, the pupils will mold themselves into worthy examples for the entire world.

WHAT IS A SCHOOL FOR

What is a school for? To make man human. Man has, in him, certain specific attributes which have to be developed and fostered so that he can rise up to his full stature. If these are ignored or allowed to lie fallow, he exists on the animal level only. Discipline alone can make him grow into his heritage. The animal is transformed by school and college into a man; or rather, he ought to be.

The teacher is the most important asset of the school. Brick and mortar do not make a school efficient and useful. Nor are books in the library or appliances in the laboratory, more essential. The teacher makes the school or mars it. He is all the books you need. He is the most desirable appliance. He shapes the manners, behavior, attitudes and even prejudices of the pupils under his care. So, his responsibility is heavy—heavier than he is aware of. The teacher dedicates himself to a great Spiritual discipline when he enters upon this profession. He has himself to be what he advises his pupils to be. The tender minds in the classroom are easily molded by his example. If the teacher speaks against smoking, he has to give up smoking. If he insists on punctuality, he has to come to the classroom on time. He is under rigorous scrutiny all the time. Any misdemeanor of his becomes the talk of the town. It is discussed during dinner in a hundred homes the same day. He has to be circumspect, all the hours of the day.

Patient effort and steady persistence are indispensable for teachers. Their task is of basic importance to the nation. Children's minds are innocent, tender and pure. The snake gourd is apt to grow curved, if left alone. So, gardeners tie a stone to its end and the weight makes it straight, as it grows longer and longer. The minds of children and of youth are also apt to grow crooked under the influence of the sensuous films, the hollow hypocritical atmosphere created by the elders, the lure of glitter and glamour and of a false sense of adventure and fame. So, school has to attach the stone of discipline and make them grow straight and true.

The stone should not be too heavy, lest it snap the gourd in two! Avoid extremes, at all times, in all cases. Disciplinary rules have to be well thought out and adapted to the age-group they wish to correct. The atmosphere must be so charged that obedience to discipline comes automatically, with full heart. Such discipline will shape good leaders for the nation. Unlike the present generation of leaders, these can inspire and guide the people along right lines. They have also to be good followers. Fine soldiers make fine generals. Young apprentices of peace become pillars of peace, champions of peace. Regulate the food habits of the children. Food determines to a large extent health and intelligence, emotion and impulse. Set limits to the quality and quantity of food, as well as the number of times it is consumed, and the timings. Recreation too has to be moral and elevating, in the company of the righteous and God-fearing.

The real purpose of schooling is ignored now by parents and teachers. Parents wish that their sons and daughters secure a University Degree, by hook or crook, because it is a status symbol. Teachers wish that a high percentage of their pupils must pass the examinations, without giving them any bother while teaching, or while not teaching! Each student is a precious trust, so far as the teacher is concerned. He should be honest, in the execution of his duties. For remember his example has a lot of influence on the class.

The schools are being established in order to guide children on right lines and to inspire the elders to be examples of tolerance, service and mutual love. Children learn at school for a few hours during a few months of the year, a few disciplines and skills, and some chunks of information. They are already shaped, well nigh irreparable by the parents, kith and kin and elders. Children admire their elders and imbibe by imitation their prejudices and predilections. They watch the behavior of the elders and value it more, though they may not follow their advice and admonitions. They can see through the veil of humbug and the paint of hypocrisy.

SCHOOL IS ASSUREDLY A SACRED PLACE

A school is assuredly a sacred place where a holy task is being put into action—the shaping and molding of the fortunes of many generations of the country. The children here learn the skills and the special aptitudes which can take each of them to the goal of happiness, which can take the families and societies, to which they belong, to peace and prosperity. Here they are corrected and trained. They are introduced to the grand culture that the ancient seers and sages of the land have discovered and laid down. I am glad I came here and met these children. I am glad that their parents, especially their mothers, have also been invited and are present. For they should know the school which their children attend and the teachers who train them, so that they may contribute their gratitude to those who share their responsibility.

Parents first, teachers next, playmates and companions later, and the leaders who command the allegiance of millions, last have all to be constantly examining themselves, whether they are fit examples to be followed by the children of the land. These shape the character, and so shape the future of the country. Elders must revere the teacher so that the child may revere him. When the teacher comes to your house, honor him, so that your child may honor and obey him. This will induce the teacher, too, to become worthy of honor. It will make him aware of his role.

Parents and teachers and even the leaders of the nation are devoid of admiration and adoration, understanding and practice of the basic principles of Indian Culture. Children are denied the precious heritage which is their due. They are inducted into alien ideals, thoughts and habits. They are praised for reciting foreign nursery songs, to the neglect of native rhymes! The educated child cuts himself away from the village child or the children of the unschooled.

Do not burden the tender brains with all sorts of lumber, bits of information that can never be put to use, facts that warp the strands of truth. Do not sow hatred or contempt of any class or caste, faith or cult in the virgin mind of the little one. What profit is it for the children to know the length of the Mississippi River or the height of Vesuvius? Why load them with information they may never require? On the other hand, give them the tonic to strengthen their spirit—the tonic of the name of the Lord, the tonic of meditating on the glory of God in the silence of the heart. Formerly, children were learning Ramanama.

Now they sing, "Ding dong bell. Puss is in the well." This type of silly meaningless jargon is spreading everywhere like a poisonous infection destroying the seeds of peace and joy.

When you relate stories to the children, select such stories as have some reference to the background of the children's home life. Tell them stories which will implant in the mind genuine disgust for evil sights, evil entertainment, evil deeds and evil habits. Tell them how they must forget the wrong done to them by others and the good that they do to others. Make them take up some positive task and the negative attitudes will fall off. Good habits will drive out bad ones. The teachers must tell the children inspiring tales of our saints and heroes and plant the love for spiritual literature.

Teachers and parents must see that children learn certain good habits and attitudes during these formative years. What is read from books must be contemplated upon, thought over in quietness, reflected upon in silence. This is a very good exercise in intellectual development and in the acquisition of mental peace. The instinct to quarrel and fight out all misunderstandings must be regulated and sublimated. Children should not enjoy the infliction of pain or be allowed to suffer physical pain or mental anguish. They must have a sense of responsibility at least for the safe custody and proper upkeep of their books. They must not take delight in showing off their dress or ornaments or status, or wealth, before the less fortunate children of the school.

AND MORE IMPORTANT THAN ALL

They have to be taught sensible habits of personal cleanliness and more important than all, the habit of prayer at regular hours. They may be encouraged to go to bed regularly every day at 9:00 p.m. Teach the children the habit of daily prayer, when they rise from bed and when they lie down to sleep after the day is over. Do so yourself. You will find that it adds calm and content. It is for their sake that you toil, it is to make them free from anxiety that you serve. You sacrifice your own comforts in order to ensure that they spend their days in comfort. The intention is legitimate, but comfort is not all. Are you practicing brotherliness, tolerance, equanimity, charity and compassion? These are the armors that guard the mind from sorrow and pain. Teachers must be vigilant to help and to encourage them to avoid any trace of dishonesty in their actions and falsehood in their statements. Selfishness, envy and egoistic pride are the three tendencies and attitudes that should not take root in the tender hearts. Prompt them to engage themselves in acts of service to others. Look at the trees. They serve us with no thought of self. They comfort all with their shade. Rivers, too, render service to all without asking for recompense. Tell the children about the services the cow offers to man.

Deprived of the help given by the three—the tree, the river and the cow—man's life becomes precarious. What a shame it is for man to behave selfishly while his life itself depends on the unselfish behavior of the rest of creation! Whatever information, instruction or inspiration man has gained, or whatever wealth, riches or material possessions he has earned he should share them with others in an unselfish manner. This is his primary duty. Teachers must be on the watch for chances to instill these ideals in the hearts of the pupils.

Teachers should not trot excuses, based on material considerations, to shirk or bypass their essentially spiritual task of "education." They must bear trials and tribulations with calm content and do their work even more efficiently. And God will reward them and society will learn to revere them, all the more, for their sacrifice. The world honors the man who suffers gladly far more than he who enjoys shamefacedly! Fundamentally, the years of life are but a short span, a rest in a wayside caravansary, a drama played on a rickety stage, a bubble upon the waters. During this fleeting hour, it has been given to a few to share this golden chance of imparting instruction, inspiring devotion, instilling courage into the growing child, so that it will be grateful to them forever.

More than all, fill your mind with God and transmit God to the children. Look forward to no remuneration or reward, except the joy on the faces of the children. Nowadays teachers are more attached to their salaries than to their duty. They are centered more on their own lives than on their sacred task. Give up the mad rush in pursuit of degrees. Pursue, rather, chances to serve others and to promote the prosperity of the nation. Indian culture has declined so far and so much because teachers, who are its guardians and promoters, are content to feed themselves and their families and to cultivate their own fame and fortune. The Vedas tell us that, not by acts, not by progeny, not by riches, but only by renunciation can Immortal Bliss be achieved. So renounce, renounce! Serve, Love and give your knowledge, your delight and your Love gladly to the children. Serve thus the society and the people.

THE WHOLE UNIVERSE IS A UNIVERSITY FOR YOU

A pass in the examination does not make a person more useful or more wise. The duty of teachers is to correct and counsel the students, charging them with enthusiasm and courage and removing their sloth and vacillation. This is the underlying object of all the curricula and classes—to eliminate narrowness of outlook and to promote wide, inclusive modes of thought, word and deed. The faith in the Oneness of all must be rooted and strong. The Upanishad declares, "All this is enveloped by God," and the Gita declares, "All this is the Lord," and "The Lord is in all beings." Consider every student as your own child who is eager to learn. Consider every subject you teach as a means for instilling faith in God. When you teach physics, lead the students into the magnificent mystery of philosophy also. While teaching botany, guide them into the sublime secrets of the tree, and of the Creator who has blessed them with it. Life is a tree. The mutual relationship we cultivate and cherish is symbolized by the branches, twigs and leaves. The thoughts arising in the mind are the flowers. Bliss is the fruit, and virtue is the sweet juice it contains. The tree is held firm by the roots which feed it, these roots symbolize faith, self-confidence.

The whole Universe is a University for you. You can imbibe wisdom from the sky, the clouds, the mountains, the rivers, the daily phenomena of sunrise and sunset, the seasons, birds, trees, flowers, the insects—in fact, all Beings and Things in Nature.

Embodiment of the Divine Self, students, you go and join schools, colleges and universities for the purpose of getting education. Do not think that the education which you should get is confined only to the colleges or schools. Education should be got from all the world over. It can be got from a workshop. It can be got from a farm. It can be got from a profession or trade. Moving in the market can give you education. All aspects of lifc can impart education. You must regard the world itself as a big university. From the time you get up from your bed till the time you go to sleep again, you are using your education for earning the pittance of a livelihood. If you cannot use your education to be near the feet of the Lord, what is the purpose of all this knowledge? You must have God in your heart and recognize all living beings as equals. You must make every effort to overcome the four .obstacles, namely lust, anger, attachment and greed. So long as these thieves are in your home, there is no certainly that you will get the treasure of wisdom. But after driving away thieves, you will get a bigger thief into your home and that thief is God Himself. That is why He has been called (Chitta-Chora) or one who steals your heart.

Why should they attend Schools and Colleges far from their homes, spending huge amounts of money? They attend schools and colleges, in order to cultivate discipline, control emotions, canalize passions. Learning is just a small fraction of what can be gained from schools and colleges. They instill into the pupils the lessons of natural cooperation, good manners, courtesy, compassion and comradeship, adjustment to limitations, overcoming of obstacles with calm deliberation. The marks you get in the tests and examinations in each subject are not so important. I attach more importance to the "remarks" that you earn—whether you are judged good, bad or indifferent, fresh, fair and free or wicked, vile and vicious.

Education

Education must include the education of the mind of man, of his impulses to hate, to hoard, to fight, to defame.

It is not merely the acquisition of certain skills, by which the materials found in nature can be reshaped into utility products. It is not merely the acquisition of information about the laws of nature. It is a process by which man makes the best of his own inner equipment, to know himself. It should open his inner eye, more than the outer.

The outer must reveal the Glory of God.
The Inner must reveal the God Within.

DAME CINEMA DAME NOVEL

The years spent by these young persons as students in schools and colleges are the most crucial years of their lives. The heart of youth is pure, clean, full of enthusiasm and optimism. They are eager to achieve happiness, earnest to serve others and enter upon an adventure. It does not involve such effort to direct them along beneficent channels. Of course with equal ease, they can be directed along maleficent channels too.

The educational system must decide to direct them to the real job, achieving of the Divinity latent in each one. Striving towards such a goal is an essential step for ensuring social, national and world peace and prosperity.

Beautiful, fruitful ideals must be planted in the tender hearts of the young. They are lovely creepers which can yield clusters of fragrant flowers, spreading the fragrance of truth and virtue. They have to be fostered with love and care, by parents, teachers and all those interested in the progress of the nation. It is a sacred responsibility which cannot be bypassed.

The years of student life must be saturated with cooperative activity, social service, tolerance, eager search for truth and readiness to sacrifice one's interests for the good of those who are less fortunate. Moral and spiritual values have to be honored as much as, if not more than, economic and material values. Life must be a harmonious blend of these values with emphasis on moral strength.

Education is no bookworm affair. The process must include the study and appreciation of all trades, professions and guilds. It must encourage the acceptance of the good and the rejection of the bad. Spiritual education is not a distinct and separate discipline. It is part and parcel of all types and levels of education. In fact, it is the very foundation on which a lasting edifice can be built. Secular and spiritual education are like the two halves in the seeds of pulses. The germ that sprouts is in between. It is fed by both.

Youth has the capacity to grow into strong, straight aspirants, who can scale the heights of spiritual adventure; but youth has no proper guidance. On the other hand, youth has evil temptation, evil example and evil advice are spread around on all sides, most attractively.

There are two evil sirens that entice them into futility and frivolity, diverting them along the paths of ruin. One of them is called, Dame Cinema and the other is named, Dame Novel. The film contaminates and corrupts. It pollutes young and innocent minds. It teaches crime, violence and greed.

It destroys the basic humanness and degrades it into bestiality.

Even ochre-robed monks are steadily dragged down to sin by its insidious influence.

Dame Novel too corrupts equally, with salacious pictures of bestiality. They both lead the young away into the wilderness of vice. They do not know, nor do they care to know, how to shape the young into self-reliant self-confident, self-knowing citizens. The vital need is ignored.

Note the type of dress that is now considered fashionable—the weird uncouth bush-shirts and drainpipe pants. Note the sideburns and the weird mustaches and beards that besmirch the face of youth. Note the value attached to slovenliness and primitivity, to foulness and frivolity. No one can appreciate this trend, except those who are victims to it. Disgust is the only reaction one gets.

When the exterior is reeking with untidiness how can the interior be tidy?

How can harmony and honesty be installed in such a cluttered heart and in such a lumbersome brain? Young people move about like clowns. They pay no attention to the seriousness of the task which lies ahead of them. When the parents, society and the nation yearn that they should become "biggers," they revel as "beggars." before the fashion fabricators of other lands, the ism-peddlers of other countries and the hysterics of other cultures.

KEEP AWAY FROM SUCH BOOKS

You must read good books. Then only can you claim to be good students. But good books are now becoming rare. Cheap books and magazines give stories of bad life, dealing with crooks and cruel men, cheats and dacoits. Keep away from such books. They will dirty the mind, and fill it with anger and hate, and mischief. Read the sacred books of your religion and of other religions. Read the *Mahabharatha*, the *Ramayana*, the *Bhagavatha*, the Bible, the Quoran and other sacred books. In some families, reading of such books is done daily. So the children know something about the sages, saints and Divine Persons of the past. Such reading is not done in most families, even the elders do not know what the books have in their pages! How then can children know?

Then again, I will advise children not to read horror comics, books on crime and sex, and novels of vice and wickedness. Avoid also films, for though they may be advertised as very educative and inspiring, the producers, in their greed for profits, smuggle in low vulgar debasing scenes in order to please raw, untrained minds. Don't allow the virus of vice to infect your brains. If that happens, you descend to levels worse than the beasts. Do not imagine that it will be possible for you to live happily without any anxiety or bother. Do not build castles in the air and hope to live in them. Life is a mosaic of pleasure and pain. Grief is an interval between two moments of joy. Peace is the interlude between two wars.

Teachers are not nowadays aware of the nobility of their profession as society has turned ungrateful. Boys and young men have the stars of the silver screen as their gods and guides. They learn deeply and dangerously from films, from horror comics and from crime books. They have no sense of values implanted in them early in life. They are carried away by the torrent of triviality. The teacher is a helpless witness of this tragedy. For, he has no strength and sustenance to impart, no ideal to implant, no enthusiasm to transfer. If only the teacher is imbued with the lessons of the Upanishads and the Gita, he can by precept and example turn the children along the path of peace and joy. Of course, the home and society must supplement his efforts and foster the impressions he is able to confer. The teacher must work in an atmosphere of Love and Truth, not hate and falsehood. He must move among the children, happy and content, not angry and sullen. Then only can he radiate Love.

Students, you are Embodiments of the Divine Self. There is a great and urgent need that you should delve into the problem of who exactly you are, and realise that you are Divine, so that you can raise yourselves to that level, instead of remaining merely human or degrading yourselves into the lower level of animality. What exactly are the degrees which you earn now, after such elaborate and exhausting studies? The degrees are only begging bowls, which you can hold while presenting yourselves in front of office after office, seeking jobs. Education does not fill you with self-confidence, self-reliance and self-knowledge. How can even parents, teachers and the elders give you these, when they are themselves suffering from their absence? Since they do not have these qualities, the country is in the throes of poverty, faction and sloth.

Education does not ensure the skills and attitudes essential to live a life of peace and contentment. It is not "full" nor does it function in a comprehensive manner, taking all the needs and goals into its orbit. It is satisfied now with cramming books, reproducing from memory, research into trivialities and awarding degrees which mean nothing special. And its products parade their purposelessness, shouting that God is dead and that virtue is a superstition. How can man exist without God, or God, apart from man? There can be no garland without the string that runs through the flowers. There can be no men without the inner kinship that God ensures for each. He is the Universal Absolute String, invisible, but inevitable.

Remember

When children are equipped with discipline to secure balance, equanimity, harmony and peace, they can no more be drawn into wild adventures and barren activities.

✣✣✣✣✣✣✣✣

LET THE CHILDREN REALISE THAT PRAYER IS UNIVERSAL

The conflict between persons who accept God and deny Him, those who declare that God is to be found in this or that place and those who affirm that He can be found nowhere, is never ending. It has continued throughout the ages. While considering this situation, one has to remember that while it is unnecessary to awaken a person already awake and easy to awaken a person who is asleep, we cannot awaken, however much we try, a person pretending to be asleep. Those who do not know can be taught, by means of simple illustration, what they do not know. But those afflicted with half-knowledge and proud of that acquisition are beyond any further education.

Some short sighted critics declare that spiritual matters should not be communicated to children, for they are too young and inexperienced to benefit by the instruction. But if a thing deserves to be done, the sooner we set about it the better. The slogan, "Start early, drive slowly, reach safely" applies not merely to journeys by road or rail. It applies also to the journey from untruth to Truth, from darkness towards Light and from death to Immortality. The unrest, anxiety, fear and hatred that torment the world now is largely due to the neglect which kept off, from the growing child, the disciplines that can regulate the passions and emotions of man. We postpone this essential task of education at our peril. For, when children are equipped with the discipline to secure balance, equanimity, harmony and peace, they can no longer be drawn into wild adventures and barren activities. You have to learn spiritual disciplines along with the information-giving subjects of the curriculum. You have to earn the high Diploma which the Upanishads offer you, namely, Child of Immortality, along with the degree MA, B.Sc., etc., which help you eke out a livelihood, up to a certain stage of life.

But remember you cannot take up the threads of spiritual discipline all of a sudden after retiring from active service! You cannot learn spiritual discipline when you are physically debilitated and overwhelmed by the approach of death. How can a man think of God, his Savior, when he himself is overcome by sorrow at the need to depart from this world and when all around him, his kith and kin are weeping and wailing loud and long?

No. Everyone must learn the secret of happiness which consists in refusing to shed tears for anything less than God.

Of course, the first duty of the schools is to instill in the minds of the young the value of prayer, of humility and loving service to others. In the homes where they grow, the parents have to be imbued with faith in the basic truths of this Universal Religion. They must be seen worshipping at the family altar, meditating in silence, forgiving the lapses of others, sympathizing with pain and grief. They should not allow the children to be worried, helpless, discontented and distressed, as if they have no God to lean upon, no inner reserves of strength and courage to fall back upon.

Let the children realise that prayer is universal and that prayer in any language addressed to any Name reaches the same God. Let them understand that God can be invoked through a picture or an idol to fulfill man's sincere desire provided it is helpful to others as well as to oneself. Love can bind all children together, for they have not yet learnt to hate. Love can, similarly, unite all mankind; provided man is cured of greed, envy, desire, and attachment.

ONLY ONE RELIGION THE RELIGION OF LOVE

But what we have to do is to place before them in sweet, simple style, the teaching of all faiths. The Sai religion is the harmonious blending, through Love, of all religion. Through some followers of other faiths feel that Sai religion is contrary to theirs, we should not entertain similar feelings. Ours is the totality, the sum. So we should not limit or restrict our vision.

There is one more point which I wish to emphasize. Some teachers have asked Me whether the Bala Vikas classes, can serve children of all faiths or whether they can admit only children of the Hindu faith. This question has arisen because the questioners do not know the very fundamentals of the Hindu Faith. There is only one religion remember, and that is the religion of Love. There is only one caste, and that is the caste of Humanity. You must be careful not to encourage or entertain the slightest trace of "difference" on the basis of religion, caste, creed or color, in the Bala Vikas classes.

In the Bala Vikas classes, you must try to have children from various faiths so that friendship between them can grow into understanding, and understanding into Love. Do not talk about differences between religions in the beginning. Rather, stress the obvious similarities so that the tender minds in your charge are not shocked or confused. Tell your pupils stories from the scriptures of all religions so that they can realize that the saints and seers of all lands are equally good and great.

Do not tarnish the spotlessly clean minds of the children by infecting them with a sense of distinction between one child and another. Impart instructions and inspiration equally to all.

Select stories from the scriptures of all faiths to interest the children in the values of a good life. Speak to them of the moral heroes of all lands, the Saints of all faiths. For they are all of the same stamp. No scripture enjoins violence or lays down untruth as a way of life. All religions extol Truth, Righteousness, Peace, Brotherhood, and Love. All saints are embodiments of service. compassion and renunciation.

You have to teach the equal validity of all faiths. Teach them, through quotations from the Bible, the ideals of Christianity. So too, use the sacred texts of Zoroastrians, Buddhism, Islam, etc. to acquaint them with the ideals held aloft by those faiths. Also tell scriptures of all religions. Do not belittle any religion or give predominance to any single religion.

The guru should point out to his pupils the common factor of good advice about human conduct contained in the scriptures of all religions. The Vedas teach that man should adore and worship God in gratitude for His benedictions. The Bible teaches that he should pray for peace and practice charity. The Quoran would have man show mercy to the suffering and to surrender his will to the All-high. The Buddhist texts teach the lesson of detachment and sense-control. The Zend-Avesta exhorts man to get rid of evil propensities and shine in his own innate Glory. The guru has to imbibe all these qualities and then teach them to his pupils by precept and example.

ON THE GLORY OF GOD IN THE SILENCE OF THEIR HEART

More than all else, the guru must equip himself or herself with spiritual discipline—a calm and quiet temper. He should be prepared to meet, without being ruffled, the buffetings of the environment. When someone inquires whether you have a calm temper do not get enraged. Some people get angrier and angrier when they are asked this. Even when you have to speak harshly to a child or a parent because all other means of bringing a point home have failed, let your heart be soft. Let it not be hardened by prejudice or hatred.

The sages of ancient India have consistently emphasized: "Live together, revere each other. Let not the seeds of envy, and hate grow and choke the clear stream of Love," is the prayer that they have taught the children of this land. Their teaching has been Unity, Divinity, Charity in thought, word and deed, from the first breath to the last. When teachers transmit this heritage, unspoiled and undiminished, to the children of the land its future as a glorious land is assured.

Many such parents do not allow their children to join the Bala Vikas classes, or to attend congregational singing and good company. If the children clamor at home that they may be permitted, they shout at them, and call them "mad." They say that religion and God are only for idlers or old senile people and that the path will lead them on to Renunciation, which is a calamity to be avoided! They reverse the very values of life. Parents must correct themselves before they try to correct their children.

Prayer is a good item to be included in the timetable. Instruct them in meditation, for a short while each day. Let that habit be inculcated even at this age. Five minutes of prayer and another five minutes of meditation will be a good exercise, whose taste itself will persuade the children to make it a habit. Silence is invaluable and pupils can be asked to practice it. See that they do not get too agitated or depressed. The pendulum will start to swing only when the clock is keyed up. Let them keep their desire under control. Do not key them up.

Learn from childhood the recitation of the Name and prayer and the practice of silence. Let children contemplate the beauties and magnificence of God's Handiwork and be filled with mystery and awe.

Lead the children along the joyous path of Truth. Let your faces ever shower smiles, springing from the bliss you earn from the faces of the children. Let them sing spiritual songs that glorify God. Do not fall into the traps of anger, jealousy and pride. You can avoid them through steady and sincere attention to the task you have undertaken. Give them the tonic to strengthen their spirit, the tonic of meditating on the glory of God in the silence of the heart. Spiritual discipline must be taught even in childhood. Man has the spring of joy and peace in his heart even as a child. Remember the tender mind has to be fed, with tenderness.

Children! Learn the best teaching of all faiths, put them into practice. Chant the name of God with your whole being. Imbibe the noble qualifies that those names represent. Purify yourselves and purify the world. That is my blessing.

BABA SAYS

Prayer is the very breath of religions; for, it brings man and God together and with every sigh, nearer and nearer.

TEACHER

The father, the mother and the teacher are the three primarily responsible, for molding the future of the country.

Teacher more than all, fill your mind with God and transmit God to the children.

You are the lamps from which these tender hearts must receive Light and Love.

The virtues you implant in them, the counsel you are providing them, the examples you place before them will remain carved in their memories and transform their outlook and behaviors in the days to come.

The things learnt during those early years stick in the memory and act subtly and silently on the growing mind to modify and purify the conduct of later years.

The teachers have to be embodiments of Love and patience.

The teacher must be vigilant to help and to encourage them to avoid any trace of dishonesty in their actions and falsehood in their statements.

The teacher must win the reverence of the pupil by showering on him his Love. The pupil must win the Love of the teacher by showering on him reverence and affection.

The teachers must be simple, sincere and straightforward aspirants, radiating joy and love.

The teacher feels that he has no duty to teach if, in a certain month, he is not paid his salary.

Students pay for being taught. Teachers are paid for the teaching they do. Money decides what is taught and how it is learnt.

"Pay and receive. Be paid and give." That is the bond between the teacher and the taught.

"Love, reverence, affection" these have no place in the transaction.

How then can education be fruitful?

Look forward to no remuneration or reward, except the joy on the faces of the children.

A bad pupil causes harm only to himself.

A bad teacher ruins the careers of hundreds.

Be steady and stable in your efforts. A guidepost which changes direction with every gust of wind adds only confusion to the confounded traveler. You have also to cultivate Love and expand your desire to do service.

Teachers are not nowadays aware of the nobility of their profession as society has turned ungrateful.

Boys and young men have the stars of the silver screen as their gods and guides. They learn deeply and dangerously from films, from horror comics and from crime books.

They have no sense values implanted in them early in life.

The teacher is a helpless witness of this tragedy; for, he has no strength and sustenance to impart, no ideal to implant, no enthusiasm to transfer.

If only the teacher is imbued with the lessons of the Upanishads and the Gita, he can by precept and example turn the children along the path of peace and joy.

The teacher need only tread on the footsteps of the great teachers of the past who transmitted their spiritual wealth to succeeding generations.

Your duty is to delve into the Inner Reality and discover the spring of joy therein, so that the exacting task of molding the children, into "children of India" will be a re-creating job for you, highly refreshing and rewarding.

Character on the other hand, must be a hundred percent perfect.

Utter the truth and tread the path of righteousness.

The teacher is the most important asset of the school.

Brick and mortar do not make a school efficient and useful. Nor are books in the library or appliances in the laboratory, more essential.

The teacher makes the school or mars it. He is the book you need; he is the most desirable appliance. He shapes the manners, behaviors, attitudes and even prejudices of the pupil under his care. So, his responsibility is heavy, heavier than he is aware of.

The teacher must be free from habits and practices which they recommend others to give up.

They should not lose temper. They should keep their emotions under control and not exhibit depression, dejection or wavering of the will.

Teachers should not form rival groups—some proud of their achievements, some envious of the praise others earn.

See others as your own brothers and sisters, for all are one when viewed as Self.

The teacher and the pupil will both be immersed in joy only when Love, that does not calculate the reward, binds them together.

When material gain is the goal, the joy is based on matter and does not thrill the mind. It cannot be pure, steady and sincere.

What you teach must, however, be imprinted on the heart, and not be stacked in the brain.

A bad pupil causes harm only to himself. A bad teacher ruins the careers of hundreds.

Teachers are the sculptors who shape the rocks into things of beauty and significance, of utility and inspiration.

The teachers study the pupil, their nature and equipment, and decide on their roles in society, their paths and the stages in their progress.

Teachers must lead lives based on upright conduct, moral grandeur and spiritual discipline.

The teachers of tomorrow are the students of today. So, cleansing of the atmosphere of the classroom is very necessary, in the interest of the future.

Teachers are reservoirs from which, through the process of education, students draw the water of life.

As teachers, you do not look forward to monetary or material benefits, and so, you have ample opportunity to make the child's heart and intellect blossom through the rays of Love.

The Vedas tell us that, not by acts, not by progeny, not by riches, but only by renunciation can Immortal Bliss be achieved. So renounce, renounce!

Serve, Love and give your knowledge, your delight and your Love gladly to the children.

Serve thus the society and the people.

The teacher must be like the sages of old, balanced, contented, quiet and calm scholars who have practiced self-control and who carry about with them an atmosphere of cool equanimity.

The sages say: "Let your teacher be your God."

For, it is the teacher who opens the inner eye and makes you aware of the wonder and beauty of the world around you.

GOD

You cannot describe God, all your attempt will fail. It is much better to make your mind clear and clean. Fill it with Love and devotion. That will enable you to have the true vision of God.

The name of God does not mean a stranger God but the Supreme God. When you call God, whatever form appears, treat it as God. Man has to worship God in the form of MAN.

God cannot be identified with one Name and one Form. All names are His, all forms are His. Your names too are His, you are His form. You appear as separate individual bodies because the eye that sees them seeks only bodies, the outer encasements. When you clarify and sanctify your vision and look at them through the Inner eye, the eye that penetrates behind the physical, then you will see others as Waves on the Ocean of the Absolute.

Accommodate all Forms of God in your heart. Do not exclude some and welcome others. Bear with those who adore Him in another Form, through another Name and acclaim Him in another language.

God is one without a second. You can adore Him according to your own fancy and pleasure. He does not change. He is not changed when the name you call Him by is changed or the Form you picture Him by is changed. So, don't condemn or

Baba Says

See God in everyone you meet, see God in everything you handle. His Mystery is imminent in all that is material and non-material. As a matter of fact, it has been discovered that there is no matter and material. It is all God—an expression of His Mystery. Derive joy from the spring.

GOD

WE CANNOT DESCRIBE GOD IN THE VOCABULARY LEARNED UPON THE EARTH

SEEK GOD IN THE DEPTHS OF YOURSELF NOT IN THE TANTALIZING KALEIDOSCOPIC NATURE prevent the preferences of another. He has as much right as you to worship God in the form he likes.

God is the Indweller in this physical frame. Be aware of Him all through life and offer all your activity, breathing, talking, walking, and speaking to Him, for it was by Him and through Him that you were able to do all these things.

Adore Him

So long as you have breath. So long as you are conscious, have no other thought than God. Have the Name of God in your tongue in your breath Ever.

Cultivate the habit of remembering the Lord with every breath. Then only can you remember Him with your last breath.

✣✣✣✣✣✣✣✣

FROM GOD TO GOD

"The tenth stanza in the fourteenth chapter of the *Bhagavad Gita* reveals that we have come from God. The Lord's utterance is: "You are an aspect of Me. You are not an aspect of Nature and the five elements. Since you are an aspect of Mine, there is no peace and joy for you till you reach and merge in Me." Just as a child cannot be without the mother, a river must seek the ocean from which it has come, the branch of a tree cannot survive separation from the tree, and a fish cannot live outside its sustaining element, water, man, who has come from God, cannot have real happiness until he returns to God.

"One devotee sang in the Kannada language thus: "Having forgotten You, I have come to this world. Leaving the Eternal that You are, I have plunged into this transient, temporary world. What joy can I reap in this clod of earth, as all joys are in You alone." We are born in this world because we have forgotten God. We have to find our way back to God, our destination, retracing the steps by which we have come. "All living beings have to go back to the source from which they came into existence." says the *Bhagavatha*. It is our misfortune that we have forgotten this vital message today. To remember the source from which we came is the essential spiritual endeavor that every man should make.

"Man who came to this earth in quest of the Self is wasting away his time in the frivolous pursuit of "anna" (material things). Animals are always busy seeking food. Man, who is endowed with intelligence, should not be content to remain like animals. He should strive to reach Reality. Food, sleep, fear and sex are common to birds and beasts. Man's life today is largely confined to these four things. Birth as a human being should be used for realizing the Divinity within and not in frittering it away in sensual pursuits. Chaitanya declared: "We have installed today on the throne of our heart vicious thoughts and feelings, instead of making it the seat of the Lord."

"It is obvious that most of us have to lead normal family life, but it is not a life in which you should be wholly immersed. It is not family that follows us all through. It is the purity that you have achieved, that stands by you in after-life. Some elders come to Swami and pray to Him to show them the way to God. What is the way? The way is journeying back to the place from which we have come. Suppose you go to a town and stay there in a hotel for a few days, you have to come back home after finishing your work in the town. You cannot live in the hotel forever, mistaking it to be your home. The phenomenal world is like a hotel to which we have come to experience the consequences of our actions in the past. The body is a room in the hotel in which we have to undergo the Karmic consequences. Our time and body should be used for carrying out the mission on which we have come. We are engaged in accumulating wealth, gold and other material possessions. It is true that we need money for leading our life in this world. But there should be a limit to the acquisition of those worldly objects. True welfare and happiness cannot be achieved without observing limits in life. An uncontrolled life reduces man to the level of the animal.

"Forgetting the primary goal of life, men are wasting their time. Time is precious. Death is dangling its sword over every head. Our life span is fast diminishing like water seeping through a broken pot, or a melting block of ice. Death overtakes many even before they realise their mission in life.

"The body is made up of the five elements.
It has to fall one day.
The Dweller in the body is eternal.
Free yourself from the delusion of birth and death.
The Dweller is indeed Divinity.

"This is the truth that all have to realise. Fulfillment in life cannot be found by indulging in eating and drinking.

"The realization of God is the goal and destiny of human life. From the moment of birth, suffering pursues man in one form or another throughout life. If in all these ordeals, one has to maintain equanimity and peace, he has to lead a righteous life, with firm faith in God. There is no need to give up the normal duties of a student or a householder. But everything that is done should be done as an offering to God. Thereby every ordinary act becomes sanctified. Love of God should express itself in the form of consecration of every action. This is my message to you on this sacred day."

—Bhagavan's discourse at Brindavan on Easwaramma Day, 6 May 1987

✣ ✣ ✣ ✣ ✣ ✣ ✣ ✣

WITHOUT GOD LIFE IS...

Anticipating the rains at the appropriate time of the year, as dictated by previous experience of himself and his forefathers, the ryot (farmer) prepares the field with plow and harrow. Then, when the rains come and soak the furrows, he sows the seeds, so that they may sprout and shoot though the soil. If he delays or desists, how can he reap the harvest? Or, if when the crop is ready for the sickle, he does not reap the sheaves and bundles them home, how can his granary be filled with the food he needs must have?

The rain is the gift of God. Man can only pray for it, and propitiate God by righteousness. The plowing, the sowing, the weeding and the reaping are the spiritual disciplines man must undertake to deserve the Grace and to get the strength to thank God for His Gifts.

Without God, life is like a school without a teacher. It is a wire with no current passing through it. It is a body with no soul. God is in us, around us and beyond us. As the air is imperceptible in the absence of breezes or of the things that it moves, so God too can be known only by His manifestation in man and beast, plant and bird, in things and beings all around us.

So too, God is present everywhere; but we can understand only that part of Him that manifests before our cognition.

God is inscrutable. He cannot be realized in the outer objective world. He is in the very heart of every being. Gemstones have to be sought deep underground. They do not float in midair. Seek God in the depths of your Self, not in tantalizing, kaleidoscopic Nature. The body is granted to you for this high purpose. But you are now misusing it, like the person who cooked his daily food in the gem-studded gold vase that came into his hands as an heirloom.

We have to experience the Bliss of realizing Him as the core of our being. Man is endowed with a sense of wonder and awe, the sense which makes him, either a participant, an inquirer into the mystery or a devout adorer. When he suppresses or ignores or bypasses this sense of wonder, he gets involved in the physical world, physical needs and physical pursuits. He starts worshipping Mammon and he strays away from the good, the just and the beautiful. He barters the Chalice of Bliss for a mouthful of dust.

Man extols God as omnipresent, omniscient, and omnipotent, but he ignores His Presence in himself! Of course, many venture to describe the attributes of God and proclaim Him to be such and such; but these are but their own guesses and the reflections of their own predilections and preferences.

Everything is held together by God's strength. God is present everywhere. You are only a means through which God is seeing everyone in this world. You are only imagining that you are seeing with your eyes but you, in fact, are seeing with God's eyes.

This world is full of God and everything that you see is God. God Himself has no Name, no form or attributes. You must have God in your heart and recognize all living beings as equal. Each one of you is a small particle in the Kingdom of God.

THE SAME GOD SHINES IN AND THROUGH EVERYONE

Who can affirm that God is this or thus? Who can affirm that God is not of this form or with this attribute? Each one can acquire from the vast expanse of the ocean only as much as can be contained in the vessel he carries to its shore. From that quantity, he can grasp but little of that immensity.

Each religion defines God within the limits it demarcates and then claims to have grasped Him. Like the seven blind men who spoke of the elephant as a pillar, a fan, a rope or a wall, because each contacted but a part and could not comprehend the entire animal, so too, religions speak of a part and assert that its vision is full and total.

Each religion forgets that God is all Forms and all Names, all attributes and all assertions. The Religion of Humanity is the sum and substance of all these partial faiths; for, there is only one Religion and that is the Religion of Love. The various limbs of the elephant that seemed separate and distinct to the eye-less seekers of its truth were all fostered and activated by one single stream of blood. The various religions and faiths that feel separate and distinct are all fostered by a single stream of Love.

The Vedas declare: God is the inner Reality of all beings. All this is enveloped by God. All this is God. The Divine principle that is in everyone is like the electric current that illuminates the bulbs before Me here, of different colors and different candle powers. The same God shines in and through everyone, whatever be the creed, color, tribe or territory. The current animates and activates all bulbs. The Divine animates and activates all.

Those who see difference are deluded. They are befogged by prejudice, egoism, hatred or malice. Love sees all as one Divine Family. When you cultivate Love. Love will remove the weeds of anger, and of malice. It will blossom into peace and calm. My teaching is love, my message is love.

GOD IS IMMANENT IN THE WORLD

The Universe around you is a pleasant garden full of charming patches of man-hued flowers filled with fragrance and nectarine elixir, each bed being a Religion which attracts the loyalty of millions of seekers. The Garden too is God. God dances in that Garden at His own handiwork, gladdening the flowers with the magic melody of the flute. Be full of joy and love. Share that joy and love with all. If you utter "God, God" and inflict pain on man, you will be spurned as a cheat. You need not call out, "God, God!" But, if you confer joy on brother man, God will respond with His Presence, though uninvited.

He is sweetness. So, the World, the Universe, which is His creation cannot but be sweet for those who recognize it as His handiwork. The world had to be used to instruct you on the glory and the power of God, so that you may seek Him and reach Him. Unless you brighten your vision with Love, you cannot see the Truth. Love helps you to see God in everyone, everyone as Divine. The World is not false, it is not a trap. It is the splendor of God. His reflection. He reflected and the World happened! It is His own Substance, manifesting as multiplicity, as latent or potent energy or matter. When activity is in accordance with awareness of the Divine in all, Righteousness is ascendant. When this awareness is befogged or belittled, dried up or deluded, then Righteousness is descendent and the Avatar appears among men!

✣ ✣ ✣ ✣ ✣ ✣ ✣ ✣

THE NAME WILL BRING HIM NEARER TO YOU

God is immanent in the world. So, treat the world lovingly, as you will treat your Master. God is the closest, the fondest, the most reliable companion. But man, in his blindness, ignores Him and seeks the company of others. God is present everywhere, at all times. He in the richest and the most powerful guardian. Yet, you ignore Him. The Lord is near, loving, accessible and affectionate. But, many do not open their eyes to the great opportunity. The name will bring Him nearer to you. Now, the Name is on the tongue, the world is in the mind and the owner of the Name is in the heart. The world and its attractions are distracting you.

The Lord is ever behind you, turn back from the world, He is face to face with you! Cultivate enough strength of mind to know its weakness and to surrender your all to the God whom you see face to face in all beings and all moments.

Believe that God resides in all beings, speak such words as would spread goodness, truth and beauty, do such acts as would promote the happiness and prosperity of all. Pray that the worlds have Peace.

God is Love, God is Peace, God is Strength. How can a person be in contact with God, and yet, be proud and acrimonious, agitated and angry, weak and vacillating? His claim to be in contact with God is only a laughable foible. It cannot be true. Pray: "Let all the people of the world be happy and prosperous. May all the worlds have peace and prosperity." So, pray for all humanity, for the welfare and happiness, the peace and progress of all countries of the world and all beings everywhere.

Expand yourselves; do not contract into your own tiny individuality. Expand into Universal Love, unshaken equanimity, and ever-active virtue. That is the Path which will bring out the Divinity in you to the fullness.

When the Love embraces humanity, we call it Daya (compassion based on love), the quality not of pity but of sympathy, sympathy which makes one happy when others are happy and miserable when others are unhappy.

Having come upon the world stage as man, one should act the role effectively. The tree is known by the fruit. The human body is the temple of God. He is installed there. Yearn for the realization of this Truth, seek to discover it and derive Bliss therefrom. That is Devotion, the path of love to God. Love the Highest, Love the most lovable; do not love anything lower.

❖❖❖❖❖❖❖❖

DON'T ASK GOD FOR ANYTHING

When his steps are towards God, man has no reason to fear; but when they are turned away from Him, fear haunts him at every turn. God is the source of highest joy. People yearn for joy, but they accept as genuine the counterfeit joy given by the senses. No one knows that Nature is but the vesture of God. There is nothing real except He.

When one chooses a life-partner nowadays, the first consideration is paid to external beauty and charm. Next the economic position is taken as the basis. How rich is he or she? How much does he or she earn? Questions like, how far they are educated, what is the social status of the families to which they belong, are asked later. Carried off by mere external frills and foppery, people enter into wedlock, and get entangled in misery or a destructive family life. The family cannot be stable if it is built on such a slender foundation. Prime importance has to be paid to the fundamental requisites of a good character, high ideals of tolerance and forbearance, love and service. When beauty fades or wealth wanes, the bond too becomes less strong.

It is same with the God whom you choose, adore, and yearn to live with. You should not choose God for the benefits He can shower on you. Do not expect God to satisfy your worldly or material ambitions; and when they are not realized, do not desert the Path towards God. "Baba, appear in my dream this night," you demand, and if it does not happen He is not Sai

Baba, he is Rai Baba (Stone Baba) and you go in search of some other God who will be at your beck and call. You must hold on to your faith, whatever might happen, success or failure, appointment or disappointment. When God, who is your very core, is irremovably fixed in your consciousness, there will be no room for elation or dejection. God is bliss, and when God is the undying spring in you, you will have bliss forever.

That is the reason why one saint advised his followers, "Do not ask God for anything. Let Him deal with you as He wills." Earn the qualifications—holiness, purity, faith, universal Love. He will approach you on foot to console, comfort and save! Purity of heart, mastery over the senses—if you have these two credentials. Grace is your right. Imagining that bliss is available in the outer world, men stray away from the inner path and are caught up in misery. They seek bliss in the family—the wife and children—-and, to keep up a standard of living for them, they take to evil ways. The fundamental flaw is their belief that the body is the be-all and end-all of existence. They ignore the Indweller, who has to be recognized, revered and responded to.

LEAVE THE RESULT TO THE ALL-MERCIFUL GOD

Take everything that happens to you as the Gift of Grace. Of course, on your part, you must act with all the skill and devotion you are capable of. Do this, with as much sincerity as you worship God. Then, leave the result to the All-powerful, All-knowing, All-merciful God. Let whatever ensues ensue! Why do you hold yourself responsible? He prompted it, He got it done, through you. He will give whatever results He feels He must!

Without grief, there is no relish in joy! The orange has a bitter rind. The bitterness guards the sweet juice from marauders. You cannot have a sweet sugary rind, for the sweet fruit, for then, it will be consumed entirely by all and sundry, then and there! The urge of the fruit is to travel far, so that the seeds may grow into trees in open spaces in the distance and not under the shade of the parent tree. The tree desires its progeny to spread far and wide. So if the rind is bitter, the eater will take it with him and travel some distance while removing it and start scattering the seeds only many paces away! You cannot keep gold safely in a gold box! You must have a steel almirah, for it! The gift of joy comes packed in the rind of grief. Do not pray God to give you only joy, that will be foolish. Pray for the fortitude, to realise that grief and joy are but the obverse and reverse of the same coin.

PRAY TO GOD FOR GOD

People determine the nature of the Divine, through the categories of logic and dialectics. But intellect cannot grasp it. Reason cannot delve into it. For both are shaped by one's prejudices and predisposition. We appreciate only what we like. We see only what we would like to see. "When prayer is answered and one gets what one desires, God is real. When they are not answered, God is a fake, a figment of the imagination!"

When you pray God for a job, or a son, or a prize, you are devoted, not to God, but to the job, to the son and to the prize. Pray God for God. Love, because it is your nature to Love, because you know nothing else, because you cannot act otherwise than Love. Expand your self, take in all! Grow in Love.

Live with Love, in Love, for Love. Then the Lord, who is the Embodiment of Love will grant you all that you need in spite of your not asking for anything. He knows. He is the Mother who does not wait to hear the moan of the child to feed it. His Love is so vast and deep, He anticipates every need and rushes with the help you must have. You are all waiting anxiously to know when I am granting you the interviews, so that you can place before Me a long lists of wishes which you have brought. These wishes go on multiplying. They never end. The fulfillment of one leads to a new series. Strive to arrive at the stage when His Will alone counts and you are an instrument in His Hands.

Dedicate yourself to God, Sudama was asked by the Lord, "Tell me what you need." He replied, "I need you and you alone," for, that includes all!

INFECT YOURSELF WITH MADNESS FOR GOD

See with the eyes of Love. Hear with the ears of Love. Work with the hands of Love. Think thoughts of Love. Feel Love in every nerve. The God of Love, Krishna, will come to you on the wave of Love and fill your hearts with Himself.

Do not cage Him in a picture frame. Do not confine Him in an idol. He is all Forms. His is all Names. He is the Reality of all beings. Infect yourselves with madness for Him instead of for the world. Someone has written a song about me, saying that I cure madness and confer madness, that I wipe tears and cause tears to flow! Yes, I bring tears of joy into your eyes and I wipe the tears of grief. I am said to make people mad and also to cure madness. Yes, I make them mad about God and about the Spiritual discipline needed for that. Madness for visualizing God is any way preferable to the madness for riches and reputation. I cure madness which makes people run frantically after fleeting pleasures and fall into fits of joy and grief. Shed tears of Bliss, not tears of grief. Yearn for Love that will bring you the Love of God, Love. I have no power mightier than that. I might change earth into sky or sky into earth, but, that Power is nothing before the power of Love that can bind the world and rule the world. Love, do not hate or harm. Love and Serve.

Do not count your tears of pain. Do not pore over your grief. Let them pass through your mind, as birds fly through the sky, leaving no trail behind; or as flames and floods appear on the screen in a picture-house, without singeing or dampening the screen.

Wake up every day, to the singing of the Glory of God; for if God does not exist, what is it that exists? Live every day, in that joy, with that inspiration as your companion.

Have it every day, immerse yourself in that discipline and imbibe the bliss. Do not fear people who call you mad! When you know and when your heart tells you that it is a joyful experience, carry on, in spite of calumny and criticism. It is better far to be mad for God than be mad for money, or wife and children.. If only more people suffer from this madness, the world will he a much happier place! It is by renunciation alone that immortality can be experienced! Renounce the petty pleasures and tread the path towards the Supreme bliss which is God. You say, "enjoy"; but it is when you "end joy," that you can really enjoy. These petty joys must end. The pursuit of tawdry tinsel should stop. Then, the mind will fix itself on the highest joy. I find here a vast ocean of piety and spiritual aspiration. When there are such large numbers of seekers in Dharwar, why is the city overclouded with anxiety and dread? Carry to every door the name of God and let the clouds be illumined by Love and Reverence. Let every street in the towns, every village in the state, ring with adoration of the Almighty, every sunrise sing Rama, Sankara or Krishna—any Name is effective, provided it is suffused with the Divine Essence, Love. Branches, twigs, leaves, flowers, and fruits may appear to be different in color, feel, taste, smell, etc., but all are products of the earth, drawing sustenance from the soil and the sun. Live together in love. Live

To a worldly man, a God-intoxicated person will appear mad and he will laugh at him for it. But to the God-intoxicated man, the worldly appear insane, foolish, misled, blind. Of all the insanity that harass man, God-madness is the least harmful, the most beneficial. The world has suffered untold damage due to its "mad" rulers and "mad" guides. But nothing but harmony, peace and brotherliness and love have come out of "God-Madness" of man!

CRY ONLY FOR GOD

Man must achieve the status of God, And who is God? Truth is God. Love is God. Peace is God. Develop Truth. Cultivate Love. Establish yourselves in Peace. You are on the road to Divinity. Become water, so that you can merge with water. If you remain oil, you cannot merge. So, develop divine characteristics. You are now in His Hands, in God's Care, but you do not realise it. This kerchief is held by Me. If my hand does not hold it, it falls. So too, if God does not hold you, you fall. Whatever you do, wherever you are placed, believe that God has put you there for that work. Do not dedicate your lives to material goods. Dedicate them to the Good and to God. Note down all the things for which you have cried so far. You will find that you have craved only for "paltry" things, for momentary distinctions, for fleeting fame. You should cry only for God, for your own cleaning and consummation. You should weep; wailing for the six cobras that have sheltered themselves in your mind, poisoning it with their venom: Lust, Anger, Greed, Attachment, Pride and Malice. Quiet them as the snake charmer does with his swaying flute. The Music that can tame them is the singing aloud of the Name of God. And when they are too intoxicated to move and harm, catch them by the neck them is the singing aloud of the Name of God. And when they are too intoxicated to move and harm, catch them by the neck and pull out their fangs as the charmer does. Thereafter they can be your play things. You can handle them as you please.

Have you yearned, have you pined, have you wept for the Lord as Thyagaraja did, for example? Have you shed tears of contrition, tears of exultation, while repeating His Name so full of sweetness and beauty; while visualizing His Form so full of loveliness and charm?

You might have wept, but who knows for what. Who knows the impulse that swept you into that sadness? Were they tears shed out of fear or greed or pride or because the Lord was not near?

The Divine is a wine that would intoxicate you. It is produced by the nectar that the Name of the Lord is saturated with. Taste it and you forget everything else. You are transformed. Man is, they say, a monkey that has lost its tail. Well, he must lose many more attributes of the monkey before he is entitled to call himself, man. He must dedicate his thoughts, words and deeds to God, and surrender to His Will. Then only is this animal entitled to become a Man, in whom the Divine is enshrined.

Until you realise that you are Divine, that God is your Core and Reality, you will have to undergo these entrances and exits. The same newspaper should not be pored over again and again, day after day. One life must be enough to know the mystery. So, at least, recognize that there is a mystery, search for the secret, and unravel it for yourself.

How can a man think of God, his Savior, when he himself is overcome by sorrow at the need to depart from this world and when all around him, his kith and kin are weeping and wailing loud and long? No. Everyone must learn the secret of happiness which consists in refusing to shed tears for anything less than God.

Ramakrishna used to cry in agony at the loss of another day without the vision of the Divine Mother. Have that yearning. Feel that sense or urgency. Seek to know now, yearn for that ecstasy this moment. Do not postpone or spend time in discussing others. Trying to satisfy the senses is a dreary desert path.

God is bound to you by the closest bonds of Love. Parents might fall out. Brother might take up arms against brother. Sister might slip away without recognizing sister. Children might not revere or even recognize their parents. Those are but "social or economic ties," they might declare. But, God will never desert you or deny you, or turn away from you.

God is the nearest, the dearest, the most loving, the most eager companion, comrade and kinsman for man.

STAY IN HIS PRESENCE

To spend some time in the Divine Presence in a fortune which is the reward of past merit. So look upon all and everything as images of the One, namely, God. Everyone, everything is His image. Feel thus; think thus; act thus. Then, there is no greed, no lust, no hate, no malice.

The same sky is over everyone's head. The same earth supports everyone's feet. The same air enters everyone's lungs! The same God brought all forth, brings up all and brings about the God of this earthly career. Live amicably, live joyful—undisturbed by faction and hatred. Doff this cloak of humanness and shine in the splendor of the Divine which is your reality. See everyone as Divine, not as the human roles they are playing.

In the Gita the Lord has declared. "I am the seen for all beings." The tree is a broad spread of leaf and flower, fruit and green. It is a fanned out system of trunk, branches, twigs! All have grown out of one single, small seed! Every fruit of that tree has seeds of the same nature inside it! So too, contemplate for a while on the magnificent multitude of life, all its rich variety of strong and weak, prey and hunter, distressed and delighted, creeping, crawling, flying, floating, walking, hanging, burrowing, diving, swimming—all this uncountable variety of created beings have come out of the Lord and each of them has in its core, the Lord again! (the Lord)! Visualize this immanent Divinity; you become humble, wise, and full of Love.

Man has not come into this world to strut about for a while on the stage, consuming food and gaily gallivanting. Man comes into the world so that he may bask in the Presence of God, through the exercise of Love and the cultivation of Love. The earth is a great enterprise, a busy factory, where the product is Love. By means of spiritual discipline, it is possible to produce Love and export it to millions and millions of people, in need of it. The more it is shared the deeper it becomes, the sweeter its taste, and the vaster the joy. By means of Love, one can approach God and stay in His Presence, for God is Love, and when one lives in Love, he is living in God. If you deny God angrily, you are drying up the springs of Love in your heart. If you declaim that God is nowhere, you are installing night in your heart and making it ready for dark schemes and misdeeds.

THROUGH LOVE ALONE

If Love is cultivated, the Love that knows no distinction between one self and another, because all are but limbs of the One Corpus of God Almighty. Through Love alone can the Embodiment of Love be gained. Here, no scholarship is needed. In fact scholarship will be an impediment, for it caters to egoism and it breeds doubts and the desire for disputation and laurel of victory over others preening themselves as learned! The Love you now have toward material objects—name, fame, wife and children, etc., should be sanctified by being subsumed by the more overpowering Love of God. Have the Love of God filling and thrilling your heart. Then you cannot hate anyone. You cannot indulge in unhealthy rivalries. You will not find fault with anyone. Life becomes soft, sweet and smooth. Shiva is depicted in the Scriptures and Puranas, as carrying a begging bowl. What is He asking from man? He is the giver. He in the person who demands. He demands only what He has given—namely a pure heart. He gave it pure. He wants it back as pure as when He gave it. He filled man with Love. He asks for that Love.

The bee hovers around the lotus, it sits upon it, sits, drinks the nectar; while drinking the sweet intoxicating honey, it is silent, steadfast, concentrated, forgetful of all else. Man too behaves like that when he is in the presence of God. The hum of the bee ceases and it is silent, when the drinking of the nectar begins. Man too sings, extol, argues, asserts, only until he discovers the flavor of the nectar. That nectar is the flavor of love. Where there is love, there can be no fear, no anxiety, no doubt, no restlessness. When you are afflicted with restlessness, you can be sure that your love is restricted, your have some ego mixed.

Be full of joy and love. Share that joy and love with all. If you utter, "God, God" and inflict pain on man, you will be spurned as a cheat. You need not cry out, "God, God!" But if you confer joy on brother man, God will respond with His Presence, though uninvited. For God is Love and when one lives in Love, he is living in God.

✣ ✣ ✣ ✣ ✣ ✣ ✣ ✣

GOD

God is the Inner Reality of All beings.

God too is a Reality, ever present in us and in every being.

God can be realized only through Love.

To reach God and to understand His Divinity, the only path that is available to us is the Path of Love.

If we want to go near God who is the Embodiment of Love

Or

If we want to understand God it becomes possible to do so only by means of love which is characteristic of God.

God is the only entity that is worth loving.

God is and can be only One no more.

He gives strength and vitality to all beings, only your ignorance must go.

He is concerned only with the sincerity and purity of your mind and heart and about how wholehearted and genuine your Love is.

God does not consider how wealthy or how learned you are.

Pray to God to illumine your mind, awaken your intelligence and be your Guru.

Without Love in the heart, God will not reside in the desert. Love is expansion and expansion is Divine Life.

God has given you "the Heart," to use in life. Return it to Him as clean and as pure as when He gave it, after using it, for Love, Peace, Righteousness and Truth.

And

For distributing them to all who came in contact with you.

All have love in their hearts in some form or other, either towards children or the poor or their work or goal.

God who in the Embodiment of Love is not confined to one place or spot.

God cannot be realized in the objective world. He is in the very heart of every being.

Train yourselves to serve God by serving man, in whom there is God installed in the Heart.

God is immanent in All Creation.

God is to be recognized in all that exists.

God is All-knowing, All-penetrating, All-pervading.

God is present in All Beings as Love.

Wherever Love is evident take it that it is God's own Love.

God is the greatest Lover of mankind.

God alone knows and decides what should happen to which and where and why. All else is powerless.

God is everywhere and in everyone. One should find God in every object.

God is immanent in every particle in the universe.

God is found through every particle in the universe. He is not bound by any limitation of space and time.

The whole universe is inhabited by Him. One should find God in every object. The clear vision can experience Him everywhere at all times.

God is ever with you everywhere.

God will be ever near, ever dear, ever ready with counsel and courage.

God is like the life-blood in the body.

He is found in every part, every single limb and muscle and nerve.

God is present everywhere, in every nook and corner of the world.

God is beyond Name and Form.

He is All Names and All Forms and yet incomprehensible and mysterious.

You have to admit that the God, whom you adore, is Universal enough to have many Names and many Forms.

Let your thoughts be concentrated on God, His Name and His Form. You will then find that you are always with the pure, the permanent, you will then derive pure and permanent joy.

You should constantly remind yourself:

I am God, I am God, I am God.

The day you see yourself as God, you become God.

LOVE IS GOD

Love is God. Everything is filled with love.

This Love can be experienced only through Love. There is no other way than Love to realise the One Who is the embodiment of LOVE.

This (Divine) Love is not something which grows in one moment and fails off on another.

This Love dwells in man as Self (the Spirit). The body has been described as the temple of God. In this temple Love is enshrined as Self. Such sacred and pure love can dwell only in a pure heart.

Fear and anxiety get entrenched in a heart devoid of love. A heart filled with love of the Divine will enjoy peace and be totally free from fear.

True Love is not a momentary feeling.

In the eternal Spirit of man Love shines as a pure and eternally effulgent Flame.

Love and Fear

As long as one is unable to understand the Principle of Love, one can never be free from fear and anxiety. The moment Love awakens, fear flees.

This is a small sample:

BABA SAYS

Love is enough to realise the Supreme.
Love which moves, flows from one heart to another, from one place to another, from one person to another and ultimately reaches the destination which is called the Grace of God.
Such love is pure.

LOVE

LOVE IS GOD

LOVE MORE AND MORE PEOPLE
LOVE THEM MORE AND MORE
INTENSELY

LOVE CAN TRANSFORM MAN
INTO DIVINE BEING

For instance, a railway passenger, who has a ticket, even while traveling by second class, is free from fear, But a ticketless traveler, even if he has got into a first class compartment, is haunted by fear of being caught and punished. Likewise, if a person has the ticket of Divine Love in his heart, he has no fear of anything in the world.

Life Is One Long Journey

In this journey if you have the pure, selfless Love of God within you, you can go anywhere free from fear and worry of any kind.

Love of the Divine is the first requirement in the march towards the realization of one's humanness. You must have one-pointedness and strength of mind.

That mind must be unwavering and the heart must be pure and unpolluted. You must fill your life with unselfish deeds.

KRISHNA'S LOVE PRINCIPLE

The Supreme message of the life of Krishna is the uniqueness of the Love Principle. This message is all that the world needs.

Krishna is the Embodiment of Love.

This love can be understood only through Love. This Love is strong, brilliant and unbreakable like a diamond. It is extremely Precious.

If you want to secure such Divine Love, your love (for God) must be equally strong. You can cut diamond only with diamond. If there is any defect in your love, it should be removed only through love.

Love begets love. Hatred can only beget hatred, not love. Jealousy beget jealousy. Anger breeds anger. Therefore, if you want to foster Love, you have to get rid of hatred, jealousy and anger.

To attain Krishna, the very Embodiment of Love,
Love is the only way.

Hence, if we acquire God's Love we can achieve anything in life.

Love is the one all-pervading element.

Everyone has to strive to make that love the basis of his life.

Love can be experienced only by Love and by no other means. The *Bhagavatha* the union of Love with Love.

GOD IS WHERE LOVE IS

This land of India is indeed a holy country, for here the sages have sought to discover the means of peaceful life, of happy life in communities of men, of a type of life that will put an end to grief. They discovered and taught the knowledge of Self, the chief component of which is Love.

God is where Love is, Love expressed as sympathy, charity, reverence, affection, sacrifice. God is Love, full of Love, Embodiment of Love, Indestructible Love, as He is described by those who have realized Him. So, He can be attained only through Love. Devotion is defined of the nature of the highest love. It is not blind love; it need not be blind Love.

I always advocate deep inquiry to strengthen the foundations of faith. Inquiry will only reinforce the springs of Love. Can there be anything more lovable than God, who is Beauty, Strength, Glory, Fame, Splendor, Wisdom in their fullest bloom? Love of God creates in man the love for all examples of His majesty, His mercy, His magnificence, His manifoldness. Ramakrishna saw in a flower His charm. He saw everywhere

His grandeur; heard from every throat His melody, His Flute-song. Even filth and wickedness are loved, for God allows them to be!

The great men and women of this land did not waste their lives in the pursuit of earthly possessions, but cast them off as encumbrances, hampering progress on the path to God.

Love is God. Live in love. People ride on elephants into wild life sanctuaries to watch elephants! Being on elephants they seek elephants somewhere else. So too, man being himself the residence of God seeks God outside himself, in the complex entanglement of Nature. See the God of your choice in all.

So you must become Love, in order to merge in Him. He is Beauty, so be beauty with no ugliness in you. Then, you can be one with Him. He is Compassion, be compassionate. Water mixes easily with water, not with oil. Oil mixes with oil only. God is sweetness. His words are sweet. His sight is sweet. He sounds sweet. He is sweeter than sweetness itself. Cultivate Love to all.

God is the source of all Love. Love God. Love the world as the vesture of God, no more, no less. Through Love, you can merge in the Ocean of Love. Love cures pettiness, hate and grief. Love loosens bonds. It saves man from the torment of birth and death. Love binds all hearts in a soft silken symphony. Seen through the eyes of Love, all beings are beautiful, all deeds are dedicated, all thoughts are innocent. The world is one vast kin.

With God you must become Love in order to merge with God.

THE MESSAGE OF LOVE

I shall leave one message for you to ruminate upon. That is the message of Love. Love is God, God is love. Where there is Love, there God is certainly evident. Love more and more people, love them more and more intensely. Transform the love into service, transform the service into worship. That is the highest spiritual discipline. There is no living being without the spark of love. Even a mad man loves something or somebody intensely. But you must recognize this love as but a reflection of the Embodiment of Love that is your reality, of the God who is residing in your heart. Without that spring of Love that bubbles in your heart, you will not be prompted to love at all. Recognize that spring, rely on it more and more, develop its possibilities. Try to irrigate the whole world with it, discard all touch of self from it, do not seek anything in return for it from those to whom you extend it. In your daily affairs, do not create factions, or revel in hatred. See the good in others and the faults in yourselves. Revere others as having God installed in them. Revere yourself also as the seat of God. Make your heart pure so He can reside therein.

I must tell you of the paramount importance of Love. God is the Embodiment of perfect Love; so, He can be known and realized, reached and won, only through Love. You can see God only through the rays of Love. Love, the one quality of Love, expresses itself as attachment to things, affection towards kith and kin, desire for objects, love in human relations, reverence towards the great, and devotion to God. Cultivate Love and all its aspects will be fed and fostered.

Love God see God, in every creature. Or, you can start with the individual and widen the circle of Love, till it envelops all Creation. Let the mind dwell ever on God. Let it see all as God. That is the Way to God, God is Love.

EVERY BEING NEEDS LOVE

Every being needs love, inhales and exhales Love. For Love is the basic breath. Everyone is the embodiment of Love. Love knows no fear and so, love needs no falsehood to support it. It is only fear that makes people warp the face of truth, to make it pleasant for those whom they fear. Love also seeks no reward. Love is its own reward. That is the sole gain, the joy of loving and being loved. When it is directed to God, it is called Devotion, Who would not love God when once he is aware of His Glory, Majesty, Might and Mercy? Love removes all egoism. The self is forgotten, it is superseded, it is transcended. Any trace of greed for gain, attachment, as it is called, degrades love into a bargain over the counter. Whatever the Loved one does or gives is satisfying to the Lover, the Adorer. A child is all love; its smile is most innocent; it has not learnt to work for gain. It has no feelings or attachment to the goods of the world. It plays with a toy for a while and throws it off the next moment. The love-full heart of the child hardens with age, because greed breeds hatred and envy.

It is only Love that can successfully carry out schemes for service and uplift. Love creates sympathy. Love will show the way, where hatred can only confound. The hours of life spent without the Light of Love are years of ruin, of dust and disease. One could as well be dead, and decay forever.

Love can transform man into a Divine Being. It helps him manifest the Divine which is his core.

Without Loving or being loved, no being can exist on the earth. Love sustains. Love strengthens. Love is the urge behind all adventure, all sacrifice, all success.

When you win the Love of God, His compassion will flow unto joy. Love gives and forgives. Ego gets and forgets. When your son steals some money from the house, you do not hand him over to the police. But when your servant steals a spoon, you have no such qualms. For, you have no love for the servant. Live without hating others, condemning others and seeking faults in others. "Doing good to others is the only meritorious act. Doing evil is the most heinous sin." When you feel you cannot do good, at least desist from doing evil. That itself is meritorious service! Do not try to discover differences. Discover unity. Creeds, castes, country of origin may differ but the inner hunger is the same for all men. Understand that the purpose of life is—to know the Embodiment of love, namely, God, through Love, and demonstrate thorough your own Love that you have know Him. The limbs of the body have to work in unison for the common purpose of sustaining the body and keeping it fit for its prime mission. If one limb quarrels with another or refuses to cooperate or help, the entire body, including the refractory limb will suffer. When you see a thorn on the road the feet move away; the eyes saw and immediately, sympathetic vibrations warned the feet. The love and cooperation between eye and feet come from the self within and the Love which is its very nature.

The spark of love in you, has to be cherished and fed so that it may reach God. Then, every being will be God, every act will be Divine. Every reaction you get from the outside world will be charged with Love and sweetened with that nectar. You love the God in all beings and the God in all beings responds with love. Love God, though tribulation may be your lot. Love Him though you are refused and rebuked. For, it is only in the crucible of travail that the metal is purified and cleared of blemish.

BURN THE LAMP OF LOVE

There is only one royal road, for the spiritual journey Love, Love for all beings as manifestations of the same Divinity that is the core of oneself. This faith alone can ensure the constant presence of God, with you, and endow you with all the joy you need to fulfill the pilgrimage to God. Before you experience the Divine in every being in the universe and in every cell and atom, you have to experience It in yourself. Each act, word and thought must be charged with that awareness.

To realise the Lord in every being, you must cultivate Love and drive out the bats that infect the dark caverns of your heart, the bats of hate, envy, and malice,

Burn the lamp of love inside the niche of your heart and then, the nocturnal birds of greed and envy will fly away, unable to bear the light. Love makes you humble. It makes you bend and bow when you see greatness and glory. An unbending person is infected with egoism of the worst type. Remember man is the only animal that can recognize and revere the great and the glorious. Let the light of Love illumine your thoughts, your words, your movements, your activities, your judgments. When you become transmuted into Love, the Lord, who is the Embodiment of Love, will reveal Himself to you, and play on the Flute, awakening your higher consciousness in the flood of universal love.

Entertain the belief that God exists in every living being. All people are your people and all your people are God's people. Regard God as Love, Living Love. God is the inner Motivator of all beings. The mirror of Love reflects the Self in you and reveals to you that the Self is universal, immanent in every being.

Love knows no fear, no untruth, no anxiety, no grief. I am Love. I shower Love. I share Love. I am pleased with Love.

I bless that you have more and more of Love to more and more Beings. Love is God. Love is Love.

MEN ARE FULL OF LOVE

Men, are full of Love. Their hearts are springs of mercy. They are endowed with true speech. Peace is the characteristic of the mind of man. That is the innate quality of the mind. In order to search for peace there is no need to go anywhere else. As gold and silver lie hidden under the earth and pearl and coral under the sea, peace and joy also lie hidden in the activities of the mind. Desirous of acquiring these hidden treasures, if one dives and turns mental activities inward, then he becomes full of Love. Only those who have so filled themselves with Love and who live in the light of that Love can be called men. Those devoid of Love are monsters, sub-humans. That holy quality of Love will not remain unmanifested off and on; it will be ever present, without change. It is one and indivisible. Those saturated with Love are incapable of spite, selfishness, injustice, wrong and misconduct. But in those who have no Love, the above qualities are always above everything else. Monsters are those who trample on Love and consider inferior qualities as important, while Men are those who consider those inferior qualities as snakes to be destroyed and Love alone as the quality to be fostered. Bad conduct and bad habits distort the humanness of man. Hearts filled with the nectar of Love indicate genuine humanity in man. By Love is meant Love which is unsullied, unselfish, devoid of impurity, and continuous.

Cultivate Love. Share that love with all. How can you give one person less and another more, when they are both the same as you? If you forget the basic Divinity, hatred sprouts; envy raises its hood. See the self in all. Love sprouts. Peace descends like dew. You are embodiments of Love. You have been sitting here since hours in the open, putting up with great discomfort, awaiting Me, eager to hear Me and see Me. I am speaking to you from this dais only to satisfy that ardor. When I sense your prema, I feel I must share it and allow you to share My Love. That is the best of all communications and communions. The mediation of words is then unnecessary.

I have come to light the Lamp of Love in your hearts, to see that it shines day by day with added luster. How does this Self Principle express itself in Man? As Love, Love is the basic nature of man, that sustains him and strengthens his resolve to march ahead. Without Love man is blind. The world, for him, will be a dark and fearsome jungle. Love is the light that guides the feet of man in the wilderness.

Love is the scarcest article today! There is no love in the home, between father and son, between husband and wife, between brother and brother.

Living has become very artificial. Men are moving in blind fear, not knowing what might happen to them at the next step. Prepare yourselves to be lamps, to guide them aright.

Be lamps of love that contain all. Then, there is no need for Prayer beads or austerity. Love will provide you the Grace of God.

LOVE IS A MUCH MISUSED WORD

Foster the tiny seed of Love that clings to "me." Let it sprout into Love for the group around you, and grow into Love for all mankind, and spread out its branches over animals, birds and those that creep and crawl, and let the Love enfold all things and beings in all worlds. Proceed from less love to more Love, narrow Love to expanded Love. Love is a much misused word.

Any positive response to the attraction is called Love. Any feeling of attachment, however trivial or transitory, is characterized as Love. We must certainly coin new words to indicate the forms of love. The attachment of parents to their children or of the children to the parents must be called affection. The responses to the attraction of sex is best described as fancy, fascination or delusion. The feeling of kinship or comradeship evokes dearness. The pleasure one gets through a sense of possession, especially of material objects can be known as satisfaction. The yearning to reach for the sublimity that lies inherent in Truth, this alone is entitled to be called by that holy word Love. For, that is the sweetest, the most charming, the most satisfying possession of Man. Love is strong and steady enough to overleap all obstacles, confront with equanimity, all changes of fortune and defeat all attempts to delay or deviate. It does not judge one incident as good and another as bad. It does not ascribe them to different agencies. Just as the Sun causes both day and night, the same Divine Will causes joy and grief. So the devotee does not wince or exult, when ill or well.

Cultivate Love, express Love. Let Love be your very breath. Let the sun of Love help the lotus of your heart to blossom. Love is my highest Miracle. Love can make you gather the affection of all mankind. Love will not tolerate any selfish aim or approach. Love towards all; live in Love. Be full of Love, taste the exhilaration that Love can confer. Man is Love embodied; he thirsts for Love and he finds real joy in loving and receiving selfless Love. You have forgotten your real nature, which is Love, and so you exude misery, hate and jealousy.

There is in everyone a spark of truth. No one can live without that spark. There is in everyone a flame of love. Life becomes a dark void without it. That spark, that flame is God, for He is the source of all Truth and all Love. Man seeks truth, seeks to know the reality, because his very nature is derived from God who is truth. He seeks love, to give it and share it for his nature is of God and God is Love.

Meditate on the truth and you will find that you are but a sparkling bubble upon the waters, born on water, living for a brief moment on water and dying upon its breast, merging in it. You owe your birth to God, you subsist on God and you merge in God. Every living thing has to reach that consummation, why every non-living thing too. So, do it now. Take the first step, purify the heart, sharpen the intellect or at least, begin the recital of the name of the Lord.

Cultivate Love. Sow the seeds of love in all hearts. Shower Love on the desert sands, let the green shoots, the lovely flowers, the luscious fruits, and the sweet harvest of nectar be earned by mankind. That is My wish, My mission, My vow.

YOU CAN CALL ME, EMBODIMENT OF LOVE!

I have not come to you to lecture, for I do no not believe in the value of mere words, however scholarly or pompous or profuse. I have come only to share with you my Love and partake in turn of your Love. It is that which I value most. That is the real gain.

Love is what the individual and the nation must cultivate now, for progress.

Love must again transform all relationships, social, economic, educational, professional, family, religious, legal and others. The father must love the child a little more intensely and intelligently. The mother must spread love to all who come within her influence, children must love the servants, etc. The sense of equality, that everyone is the repository of the Divine Essence must transmute social and individual behavior.

When this Love is established, no one will compete with another or look down on another.

The bond of love will knit all into a rare type of family which knows only one will and one direction.

The Lord is a Mountain Of Love, and any number of ants carrying away particles of sweetness cannot exhaust His Plenty. He is an Ocean of Mercy without a limiting shore. Devotion is the easiest way to win His Grace and also to realise that He pervades everything, in fact is everything!

I exhort everyone to cultivate Love, for I am Love, and when you manifest Love, you are only expressing Me, the Indweller of your Heart.

Therefore, O Embodiments of Love, resolve today to enshrine Love in your hearts, to cultivate it; make it universal, free from selfish desire. Become Embodiments of Love.

LOVE CAN TAME EVEN THE MOST FEROCIOUS OF BEASTS

The Lord is Love, Love—unsullied, inexhaustible, universal. He has no predilection or prejudices. Love can transform man into a Divine Being; it helps him manifest the Divine which is his core. The Divine can be grasped only through love, faith and spiritual discipline surcharged with Universal Love.

Love can tame even the most ferocious of beasts.

It prompts man to fill the world with joy and to partake of that joy. It implants a deep distressing thirst for that exultation, that elevation of the spirit.

The weapon of Love will disarm every opponent. Love begets Love. It will be reflected back, it will have only Love as reaction. Shout:

"Love"

the echo from the other person's heart will also be:

"Love."

The power of Love is infinite. It can conquer anything. Once while Lord Buddha was journeying, he was confronted by a demoness who threatened to kill him. Smilingly, Buddha said: "You are not a demon; you are a deity! I love you even if you behave like a demon." Hearing these loving words the demoness turned into a dove and flew away. Love can change the heart of even an inveterate enemy. It is this kind of universal love that should be cultivated by everyone.

Fill the heart with Love, and distribute that Love to all. Love grows with every gift of Love; the heart that pours out love is ever full. God is there, as Love and you are only drawing on Him, when you are sharing Love with others.

Therefore, turn your vision from the outer universe into the Inner Glory, the inner splendor, which you really are.

LOVE

God is where Love is.

God is Love. God is none other than the Self. So He can be attained only through Love.

God is the very Embodiment of Love.

There is no other way than Love to Realise the One Who is the Embodiment of Love.

There is nothing greater than Love on earth.

Love must flow to everyone from the Heart.

Hearts filled with the Nectar of Love indicate genuine humanity n man.

By Love is meant Love which is unsullied, unselfish, devoid of impurity and continuous.

Your own heart shining with Love is God's Love.

Love can transform man into a Divine being. It helps him manifest the Divine which is his core.

Love is present equally in all human beings as the one effulgent Divine quality.

Love is the Form of the Divine and God can be realized only through Love.

Love alone can reveal the Divinity latent in all.

Love towards All at All times.

Love is My Form. The Love that is manifest in all things equally believe that the same Love is the Over-self.

The Over-self is in everyone as the form of Love.

Love, Love alone can bind you to others and to God, who is the Embodiment of Love.

The Lord is All Love; so He can be seen only through Love.

Share Love with all, earn the treasure of Love.

Fill the heart. The one thing you should practice and that you should have in your heart is Love.

Store it in your heart, invite all to share in it.

The best way to Love God, is to Love all.

Love is everything, Love helps you to see God in everyone.

Love all, respect all, serve all.

Above all, cultivate Love towards all.

The language of Love is understood and spoken by all hearts.

Love alone is the Sine qua non. Love all beings actively.

Regard Truth and Love as the two eyes of every person. If we have these two eyes, we can master the world.

If we drink the Nectar of Love and Truth, we do not need anything else to sustain us.

If we are to earn the Love of the Lord, we have to Love everyone.

True love is not a momentary feeling.

Without loving or being loved, no being can exist on the Earth.

Love is the bridge which helps passage from Birth to Deathlessness from Death to Birthlessness.

When you rise from human-ness to God-ness then there is no more birth or death.

Liberation happens when you Love every being so INTENSELY that you are aware only of ONE. Soak your heart in love.

Yearn for the Love that brings you the Love of God.

Fill the mind with Love. Walk steadily and silently towards the goal—merging with God.

Love is the impelling force for both bondage and liberation.

Love is the means of developing devotion and achieving liberation, apart from other thing.

Love is the spontaneous nature of those who are ever in the awareness of the Self.

The Love which has the Self as its basis is pure and sublime.

The Self when it is believed in as the core of everyone will produce sympathetic vibrations in you, so that when the other is happy, you are happy, and when he is in misery, you feel it to the same extent.

That is Love, Love at its highest and sincerest.

This Love, when you cultivate it, will remove the weeds of anger and malice.

It will blossom into peace and calm.

My teaching is Love, My message is Love.

My activity is Love, My way of living is Love.

Love is a pure quality.

Love, since you must. Love for Love's sake.

Love knows no fear no untruth, no anxiety, no grief.

I AM LOVE

Where there is Love, there is Bliss.

Love is Only One
Love is Eternal
GOD IS LOVE
LIVE IN LOVE

"Do not tell me that you do not care for spiritual bliss, that you are satisfied with delusion and are not willing to undergo the rigors of sleeplessness. Believe me, your basic nature abhors this dull dreary routine of eating, drinking and sleeping. It seeks something which it knows it has lost: inward contentment. It seeks liberation from bondage to the trivial and the temporary. Everyone craves for it in his heart of hearts. And it is available only in one shop: Contemplation of the Highest Self, the basis of all this appearance.

However high a bird may soar, sooner or later it has to perch on a tree top, to enjoy quiet. In the same manner a day will come when even the most willful, the most unbelieving, the most haughty and even those who assert that there is no joy and peace in the contemplation of the highest Self will have to pray: 'God! grant me peace and consolation, strength and joy.'"

—BABA

GLOSSARY

Anasuya - Wife of the Sage Atri, in the *Ramayana* mother of Dattatreya.

Atri - A sage, and author of many Vedic hymns.

Brihadaranyaka - One of the ten Upanishads. This section deals with the teachings of Yajnavalka on spiritual Truth imparted to Janaka.

Bhagavad Gita - The Song of the Divine. It is not merely a dialogue between Krishna and Arjuna. It is an endless dialogue between the human and the Divine in the hearts of all human beings.

Bhagavatham - Is the story of the beginning-less, the ending-less Self.

Bharadwaja - A sage mentioned in the Purana.

Buddha - "The Enlightened One." Born as Prince Siddhartha. He renounced the world to become one of the great spiritual teachers of all time, and the founder of Buddhism.

Chaitanya - The name of a great devotee of the Lord. He emphasized the path of Divine Love for the realization of God. He is also known as Gauranga, and Krishna Chaitanya.

Chadramati - An Empress, welcomed every disaster as but one more example of the loving interest that the Lord had in her progress toward His Feet.

Choodala - She was the wife of King Sikhadhwaja, she was the perfect wife, learned, benevolent and was above all a great Yogini (woman yogi).

Dhruva - A saint in Hindu Mythology.

Dattatreya - The name of a great Hindu saint. Son of Atri and Anasuya.

Devaki - The mother of Lord Krishna.

Durga - Another name of Parvathi, consort of Lord Shiva.

Dasaratha - King of Ayodhaya, father of Sri Rama.

Gargi - A great scholar, she was revered in the assembly of Vedic scholars for her mastery of the abstruse problem of the spiritual voyage into the heights of Self-realization.

Ganga - The Ganges, a sacred river in India which rises in the Himalayas and flows into the Bay of Bengal.

Harischandra - A King of the Solar-race, He was famed for His adherence to Truth.

Janaka - Father of Sita. He was both king and Sage being known by the well-deserved title of Raja-rshi or Royal Sage.

Kausalya - The eldest wife of Dasaratha and mother of Sri Rama.

Mahabharata - The great Epic of India, the epic of the Pandavas and Kauravas Princes.

Maitreya - The wife of the sage Yajnavalkya. She was indifferent to worldly happiness, she asked her husband, whether riches will help her to realise the Truth and achieve Immortality. When she was told that they were hindrances and not helps, she refused to be burdened.

Mahadeva - The great Lord, name of Lord Shiva.

Maharshi - A great Sage or seer of Truth.

Markandeya - A Sage. He was remarkable for his austerities and great age, he is called "the long lived."

Mirabai - Mystic poetess, renowned for her devotion to Sri Krishna. She renounced the world and lived a dedicated life at Brindavan.

Nalayani - Was the wife of Sage Mandgalya even though she was young and He was old. Nalayani was very chaste. The Sage became very old, gray-haired. He was always in an angry mood. Still Nalayani stuck to Him as a chaste, loving and dutiful wife.

Nanda - Foster father of Lord Krishna.

Navarathri - Is the festival to commemorate the Victory of Good over Evil.

Prahlada - A great devotee of Vishnu whose life is described in the Purana.

Parvathi - Consort of Shiva. Mother of the Universe

Radha - Sri Krishna's greatest devotee. She was the embodiment of Shakthi itself and Divine ecstasy.

Rama - An Incarnation of the Lord, celebrated in the Ramayana.

Ramayana - The life-story of Rama, a celebrated epic poem by Valmiki.

Ramakrishna - A sage from Bengal. He asked His devotees to perform their worldly duties with one hand while holding to God with the other and praying to God to make their duties fewer and fewer so that at the end they might cling to Him with both hands.

Sabari - A female hermit. A devotee of Rama. Rama was so very pleased with her pure devotion that He offered her salvation.

Savitri - The wife of Satyavan. She in regarded an the "beau-ideal" or highest pattern of conjugal fidelity.

Sankara - Shortened from Sankaracharya. One of the greatest philosophers of India. An exponent of Advaita Vedanta.

Sita - Wife of Sri Rama and mother of the twins Lava and Kusa.

Sulabra - An ascetic and spiritual heroine.

Sudama - The real name of Kuchela, who was the friend of Lord Krishna in boyhood.

Upanishad - Offer Eternal Truths which ennoble and elevate the mind.

Vedas - Scriptures. Can lead man into the Vision of the Truth unreachable by the senses and unrelated to the material world. It is inaccessible to human reason because it is transcendent.

Yashoda - Foster mother of Lord Krishna.

Yoga - Union of the individual soul and the Universal Soul; also the method by which to realize this union.

Yogi - One who practices yoga.